THE ART OF MAKING
GOOD COOKIES

THE ART OF MAKING

MAKING

GOOD COOKIES
PLAIN & FANCY

ANNETTE LASLETT ROSS

AND

JEAN ADAMS DISNEY

DOUBLEDAY & COMPANY, INC., GARDEN CITY, NEW YORK

For Chuck and Gina

Contents

Recipes whose titles appear with initial capital letters in the text may be found by consulting the Index.

Have a Cookie!

The invitation to "have a cookie" extends from the days of a toddler's first steps to as long as appetite continues. Nothing in sweets can match the satisfaction or versatility of this toothsome bit. Some sweet, some plain, some grand, some fanciful as a pastry chef's hat—cookies serve many purposes.

This collection of cookie recipes is arranged to give the cookie maker a quick appreciation of the varieties included. Listed by type of cookie, each recipe indicates its place—plain or fancy—in the realm of food service.

This is not to say that a cookie labeled "plain" would not be a perfectly delightful finish to a company meal or that a "fancy" version could not go happily into a picnic basket. The contrasts of flavors, textures and colors are of foremost consideration in menu planning and the chosen cookie will reflect this evaluation.

The authors have suggested by the several chapters occasions on which cookies are needed and proudly served. Although some recipes are of such great popularity that they could have gone into each section, they of course appear only once. A list of such recipes is given with each chapter.

Each chapter's sub-index of cookies under the "plain" and "fancy" headings provides a rapid appraisal of that chapter's recipes. When a real search is on for a special cookie, the cook will do well to consult the main index.

Best wishes for good baking and good eating.

ANNETTE LASLETT ROSS

JEAN ADAMS DISNEY

THE ART OF MAKING
GOOD COOKIES

What You Should Know about Cookies before You Begin

BAKING—Use flat cookie sheets with low sides or no sides. High-sided pans prevent proper browning. Use only light-colored, shiny pans. Dark or discolored pans cause cookies to burn on the bottom. There should be 2 inches from edge of pan to each side of the oven. Too large pans prevent proper heat circulation which is necessary for even baking.

For best results, bake only one cookie sheet at a time on the baking shelf that is slightly below center of oven.

Take cookies off sheets while hot and cool on cake rack. If some cookies (particularly those with a high ratio of sugar) tend to cool and stick to pan, return sheet to oven and reheat slightly. Very rich cookies with a large amount of butter should be cooled on paper towels laid over rack.

Rich cookies should be baked on an ungreased baking sheet. For other cookies, grease cookie sheet lightly. Too much shortening on cookie sheet causes excessive spreading. Use shortening or oil on cookie sheet in preference to butter and margarine, which scorch more readily.

STORAGE—All cookies should be thoroughly cooled before storing. To keep soft or chewy cookies from becoming hard, store in an airtight container. To keep crisp cookies from becoming limp, store in a loosely covered container in a cool, dry place.

FREEZER STORAGE—Any baked cookie may be frozen, although meringue types and macaroons become a bit chewy and less crisp. Cool thoroughly, then wrap in any moisture-vaporproof packaging or bags. Cookies thaw almost immediately and can be served within a few minutes after removal from the freezer. To freshen, heat in 325-degree oven 5 minutes.

Crisp cookies, particularly, need to be protected against breakage. A coffee can, cardboard box or any firm container is an aid. Wrap cookies in moisture-vaporproof bags before placing in the container or overwrap the container with freezer paper, sealing it carefully.

Frosted cookies are best frozen on cookie sheets and then packaged to prevent icing from sticking to packaging. When thawing arrange cookies, while still frozen, on platter or tray so that the frosting will not soften in the package.

Cookie doughs of certain types may be frozen, although it usually is more convenient to have the cookies frozen in baked form so that they are ready to serve at a moment's notice. Butter-cookie doughs, refrigerator doughs and the more durable types of rolled and drop cookie doughs freeze satisfactorily.

Dough should be packed into freezer containers or, in the case of refrigerator cookies, wrap the rolls of dough in freezer paper. Allow 3 to 6 hours before baking dough, letting it thaw in the refrigerator. Once thawed, bake dough as you normally would. Thawed dough should all be baked within 24 hours of thawing, since freezing makes it more susceptible to spoilage.

Do not freeze doughs that contain large amounts of egg

whites or doughs that are highly spiced. The latter often undergo a flavor change during freezing.

Baked cookies may be stored in the freezer 2 to 6 months and retain their freshness, if properly packaged.

Unbaked cookie dough should be stored no longer than 2 months.

Substitutions—Proceed with Care

All recipes have been perfected with the ingredients specified. However, there are some variations that may be made successfully. Others will cause failure. These rules tell which are which!

FATS—If a recipe calls for butter specifically, that particular cookie is best made with butter and not a substitute. Either flavor or texture will be impaired. If, for dietary reasons, you wish to use margarine or shortening, we suggest choosing one of the many recipes calling for either of these fats. *Never* substitute oil for solid shortening of any kind or vice versa.

EGGS—*Never* substitute for eggs. There are a number of eggless recipes in the book if you need them for a restricted diet. Check in the index among the various butter cookies, molasses cookies, shortbreads and no-bake cookies.

SUGARS—Brown sugar, firmly packed, may be substituted for granulated sugar or vice versa. *Do not* substitute in recipes calling for powdered sugar. *Never* substitute synthetic sweeteners for sugar in cookies or frostings.

FLOUR—In recipes calling for cake flour, you may substitute all-purpose flour, using 2 tablespoons less per cup of the amount specified.

LIQUIDS—Coffee, fruit juices or other liquids may generally be used successfully for all or part of the liquid in a recipe. Evaporated milk, diluted with an equal part of water, may be used in place of fresh milk, as may liquefied powdered milk. *Never* substitute in recipes calling for sweetened condensed milk.

CHOCOLATE—In recipes calling for unsweetened bar chocolate, you may substitute cocoa, using 2½ tablespoons cocoa and 1½ teaspoons additional fat for each square of chocolate.

SPICES—Salt and flavorings may be omitted from any recipe for dietary reasons or taste preferences. Any favorite spice or flavoring may be added to any recipe at whim. When experimenting with various flavor combinations try to "taste" them in your mind to be sure that the combination will be harmonious.

OPTIONAL—In any recipe, nuts may be added or omitted at will except when they are a major ingredient, such as in a nut cookie, in which case their omission leaves a bland, textureless cookie. This is also true of dried fruits, such as raisins, chopped dates or figs, and of grated coconut, grated orange or lemon rind, ready-to-eat cereals and chocolate chips. If the amount called for is more than ½ cup, then do not omit the ingredient in question. In a recipe using 2 to 3 cups of flour, about ½ cup of dried fruits or nuts may safely be added. This is true for other items mentioned above, except, of course, for the grated rinds. A teaspoon and a half of orange or lemon rind gives sufficient flavor to a standard-size batch of cookies.

With any other substitution, follow the good old rule, *"If in doubt, don't!"*

Cookies at Home

Though a woman's work may never be done, there are few tasks so pleasant or rewarding as keeping the family cookie jar supplied. Besides bringing pleasure to other members of the family, it is a blessing to busy mothers to know there are delicious cookies to go with fruit or a simple pudding that will give a "leftovers meal" a happy ending.

Nor will Dad need to leave a sinkful of dishes dirty after fixing a midnight snack if there are cookies to go with milk before he goes to bed. For the always starving children, cookies are a happy solution, regardless of the time of day.

This is particularly true if you let the cookies carry their share of supplying part of the family's daily vitamin and mineral needs. If yours is a cookie-loving family, it is important that they be considered as food and not just a frill, for cookies can supply essential vitamins and minerals, if the recipes you choose to bake are selected with this thought in mind. This chapter has such recipes, although it contains ones of a more frivolous nature, too. The latter seem to belong in this chapter because they fit family needs so well or are ones that have been tremendously popular with all ages.

Some fill a dual role admirably—the fruit-filled varieties, for instance, seem both very special and yet provide important nutritional benefits. Others that are especially worthwhile

COOKIES FOR DESSERT

A variety of fillings and toppings and cookies can stand alone at dessert time. For a real spree, serve an assortment of cookies and toppings and let everyone create his own goodies.

Peanut butter cookies filled sandwich-style with jam are one delectable combination.

Crisp molasses cookies with peanut butter fillings are another.

Date or other fruit bars, cut double-size and topped with a swirl of cream cheese and orange marmalade, are elegant enough for company.

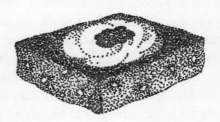

nutritionally are those with oatmeal or other cereals and those with molasses.

Aladdin Cookies deserve special mention. Not only do they contain vitamin-laden cereal but it is in cooked form, so that the recipe is a delicious way to use up cereal left over from breakfast.

Rye Drops should be rated as outstanding. These cookies are deep-fat-fried and almost a cross between doughnuts and cookies. If your family likes the flavor of rye flour, they'll love these. Wonderful with coffee around the clock.

To keep the cookies good to the last, store the soft, chewy kinds in airtight containers. Crisp ones should be loosely covered in a cool, dry spot. (There are more details about baking and storing in the preceding chapter.)

Of course, any of the icebox cookies to bake as needed are at the top of the list in convenience. Another solution to the problem of "instant" cookies is to bake one of the extra-big quantity batches and package the cookies by the dozen in the freezer. Or make up your own cookie mix to have handy for baking an extra-quick batch. Both the quantity recipes and the make-at-home mixes are in the chapter entitled "Four Score or More."

You'll also find that any of the plain varieties of bar cookies are quickly made, since they save the time of rolling, cutting or individually dropping cookies onto cookie sheets.

If you choose some of the more spectacular kinds, cookies can star at dessert time rather than just accompany fruit or ice cream. Date Bars, for instance, cut into extra-big squares and topped with icing or an orange or lemon sauce, make a good dessert. Matrimonial Bars, Coconut Dream Bars, Pineapple Bars and similar layered bar cookies are others you may wish to serve this way. The latter need no adornment at all.

And don't overlook the idea of making cookie sandwiches

with the big, crisp rolled cookies put together with icing, ice cream, cream cheese, jam or the children's favorite, peanut butter.

In this chapter are receipes for these Good Cookies:

PLAIN   FANCY

BALL

Chocolate Snaps   *Chocolate Oatmeal Balls*
Ginger Mounds

BARS

Brownies I   *Pineapple Bars*
Butterscotch Bars
(Blond Brownies)
Chocolate Crispies
Date Bars I
Toffee Bars

DROP

Aladdin Cookies   *Brown Sugar Nut Crisps*
Banana Nut Cookies   *Chocolate Nut Drops*
Buttermilk Sugar Wafers   *Peanut Crunch Cookies*
Chocolate Chip Cookies   *Rye Drops*
Ginger Crinkles
Molasses Cookies
Oatmeal Crisps
*Peanut Butter Chocolate
    Chip Drops*
Potato Spice Drops
Soft Oatmeal Cookies
Sour Cream Crisps
Sugar and Spice Drops

PLAIN   FANCY

FILLED

Date-filled Drop Cookies
Georgia's Briars

ICEBOX

Coconut Wafers
Nut Thins
Oatmeal Crisps
Peanut Butter Crisps
Spiced Sour Cream
   Cookies
      Plain Variation

NO-BAKE

Chocolate Crisp Bars   *Coconut Fruit Balls*
Fudgies
Peanut Butter
   Crispies

PRESSED

Butterscotch
   Cookies

ROLLED

Chocolate Oatmeal
   Wafers
Rolled Chocolate Dollars
Rolled Oatmeal Wafers
Spiced Cream Cookies

Other recipes that could be included in this category are the following (to locate, see index):

BALL
Lemon Raisin Treats
Sugar Oil Balls
BARS
Quick Unbaked Brownies
DROP
Cereal Crunchies
Chocolate Drops
Hermits
Mincemeat Drops

ICEBOX
Basic Icebox Cookies
NO-BAKE
Peanut Butter Drops
ROLLED
Fruited Bars
Hildur's Gingersnaps

BALL COOKIES

Chocolate Snaps [PLAIN]

Sugar-dusted

½ cup shortening
1⅔ cups sugar
2 eggs
1½ teaspoons vanilla
2 ounces or squares unsweetened chocolate, melted

2 cups sifted all-purpose flour
1½ teaspoons baking powder
½ teaspoon salt
5 tablespoons milk
⅓ cup sifted powdered sugar

Cream soft shortening with sugar. Blend in eggs and vanilla. Add melted, cooled chocolate, mixing thoroughly. Sift together dry ingredients and add alternately with milk. Chill dough 4 to 6 hours. Form in small balls. Dip in powdered sugar. Place on greased baking sheet, allowing room for spreading. Bake at 375 degrees 12 to 15 minutes. *4 dozen*

Chocolate Oatmeal Balls [FANCY]

Nut-garnished

¾ cup shortening
1 cup brown sugar
2 ounces or squares
unsweetened chocolate,
melted
½ teaspoon salt
½ teaspoon baking powder

1½ cups sifted all-purpose
flour
1½ teaspoons vanilla
¼ cup milk
1½ cups rolled oats
1 cup chopped nuts for
garnish

Cream shortening until soft. Blend in sugar gradually. Add melted, cooled chocolate. Sift together dry ingredients and add alternately with milk and vanilla. Work in rolled oats, kneading dough with hands if necessary. Form in walnut-size balls, topping each with chopped nuts. Bake on lightly greased cookie sheet at 350 degrees 12 to 15 minutes. *3 dozen*

Ginger Mounds [PLAIN]

Expect requests for more

¾ cup shortening
1 cup sugar
¼ cup molasses
1 egg
2 cups sifted all-purpose
flour
¼ teaspoon salt

1 teaspoon baking soda
1 teaspoon baking powder
¼ teaspoon cloves
1 teaspoon ginger
1 teaspoon cinnamon
½ teaspoon nutmeg
¼ teaspoon allspice

Blend soft shortening and sugar together. Stir in molasses and egg. Sift together dry ingredients and add in about three portions. Chill dough 1 hour. Form walnut-size balls of dough. Dip in granulated sugar. Place on lightly greased sheet 2 inches apart. Bake at 375 degrees 8 to 10 minutes. *5 dozen*

BAR COOKIES

Brownies I [PLAIN]

Chewy fudge bars

½ cup butter or margarine
1 cup sugar
2 eggs
2 ounces or squares
   unsweetened chocolate,
   melted

½ cup sifted all-purpose
   flour
¼ teaspoon salt
½ cup broken nut meats
1 teaspoon vanilla

Cream butter and sugar well. Add eggs, then melted, cooled chocolate. Stir in sifted dry ingredients, nuts and vanilla. Bake in 8-inch-square greased pan at 325 degrees about 40 minutes. Cut in squares when cool. *2 dozen*

Butterscotch Bars [PLAIN]

Fine for lunchboxes—also called Blond Brownies

1 cup brown sugar, firmly
   packed
¼ cup butter or margarine
1 egg
¾ cup sifted all-purpose
   flour

1 teaspoon baking powder
¼ teaspoon salt
1 cup coarsely broken nut
   meats
1 teaspoon vanilla

Melt butter and brown sugar, stirring until sugar is dissolved. Cool to room temperature. Add egg. Sift together dry ingredients and add with nuts and vanilla. Spread into greased 8-inch-square pan. Bake at 350 degrees about 25 minutes. Cool on rack 10 minutes, then cut into squares. *2 dozen*

Chocolate Crispies [PLAIN]

Thin and crisp bars

1 cup sifted all-purpose
   flour
½ teaspoon baking powder
¼ teaspoon baking soda
¼ teaspoon salt
1 cup sugar

2 ounces or squares
   unsweetened chocolate,
   melted
3 tablespoons butter
2 eggs
1 teaspoon vanilla
¾ cup finely chopped nuts

Sift together dry ingredients. Combine melted and cooled chocolate with butter and blend well. Add eggs, vanilla and then sifted dry ingredients. Fold in nuts. Pour into 9 × 13-inch pan lined with waxed paper. Bake at 375 degrees 12 to 15 minutes. Cut into squares while hot, remove from pan and cool on rack. *32 squares*

Date Bars I [PLAIN]

Cake-like

2 eggs
1 cup sugar
2 tablespoons butter,
   melted
1 cup sifted all-purpose
   flour

1 teaspoon baking powder
1 teaspoon cinnamon
¼ teaspoon salt
1 cup cut-up dates, pressed
   down
½ cup finely chopped nuts

Beat eggs with sugar until smoothly blended. Stir in melted butter. Sift together dry ingredients, then add with dates and nuts. Pour into greased 9-inch-square pan. Bake at 350 degrees about 30 minutes. Cut into squares while warm. Cool and roll in powdered sugar. *2 dozen*

Pineapple Bars [FANCY]

Dessert favorite

1 cup sifted all-purpose flour	½ cup shortening
½ teaspoon baking soda	1 cup rolled oats
½ teaspoon salt	⅔ cup drained, crushed pineapple
⅔ cup brown sugar	½ cup light seedless raisins

Sift together dry ingredients. Add room-temperature shortening, then oats and pineapple. Beat until well blended. Add raisins. Bake in 9-inch-square pan at 350 degrees 25 to 30 minutes. *3 dozen small bars*

Toffee Bars [PLAIN]

Coffee-flavored

¼ cup melted butter or margarine	1 teaspoon baking powder
1 cup brown sugar	¼ teaspoon salt
1 egg	1 teaspoon vanilla
1 cup sifted all-purpose flour	¼ cup cold, strong coffee
	½ cup broken nut meats

Stir brown sugar into melted butter until dissolved. Cool. Add egg. Sift together dry ingredients and add alternately with coffee and vanilla. Stir in nuts. Bake in greased 9-inch-square pan at 350 degrees about 30 minutes. Cut into squares while warm. *3 dozen*

DROP COOKIES

Aladdin Cookies [PLAIN]

Made with cooked cereal

⅓ cup shortening
1 cup brown sugar, packed firm
1 egg
1 cup cold, cooked rolled oats or other cooked cereal
1¼ cups sifted all-purpose flour

½ teaspoon salt
½ teaspoon baking soda
1 teaspoon cinnamon
½ teaspoon nutmeg
½ teaspoon ginger
1 cup seedless raisins
1 cup chopped nuts

Cream shortening and sugar. Add egg and cereal. Sift together dry ingredients and stir in, then add raisins and nuts. Drop on lightly greased cookie sheet. Bake at 400 degrees 12 to 15 minutes. *4 dozen*

Banana Nut Cookies [PLAIN]

Soft in texture

1½ cups sifted all-purpose flour
1 teaspoon baking powder
¼ teaspoon baking soda
½ teaspoon salt
1 teaspoon cinnamon

¼ teaspoon nutmeg
1 cup sugar
½ cup butter or margarine
2 eggs
1 cup mashed ripe banana
1½ cups rolled oats

Sift together flour, baking powder, soda, salt and spices. Add sugar, butter (must be room temperature), eggs and banana. Beat until smooth. Fold in rolled oats. Drop on lightly greased baking sheet. Bake at 375 degrees 12 minutes. *4 dozen*

Brown Sugar Nut Crisps [FANCY]

Delicious ice cream accompaniment

1 cup brown sugar, firmly packed
1 egg
1 tablespoon butter
2 tablespoons flour
1 cup finely chopped nuts
¼ teaspoon salt
1 teaspoon vanilla

Beat together brown sugar, egg and butter until well blended. Add flour, nuts, salt and vanilla. Drop by small spoonfuls on greased and floured baking sheet. Bake at 350 degrees about 10 minutes. Cool slightly before removing from cookie sheet. *2½ dozen*

Buttermilk Sugar Wafers [PLAIN]

Ever so good

½ cup soft butter or margarine
1 cup brown sugar
1 egg
2 cups sifted all-purpose flour
½ teaspoon baking powder
½ teaspoon baking soda
¼ teaspoon salt
¾ cup buttermilk
1 teaspoon vanilla

Cream butter and sugar well. Add egg and blend. Sift together dry ingredients and add alternately with buttermilk. Add vanilla. Drop on lightly greased baking sheet. Bake at 375 degrees about 10 minutes. *4 dozen*

Chocolate Chip Cookies [PLAIN]

Standard favorite

⅔ cup butter or margarine
1 cup brown sugar
½ cup white sugar
2 eggs, beaten
2¼ cups sifted all-purpose
   flour
½ teaspoon salt
1 teaspoon baking soda

1½ teaspoons vanilla
1 cup chopped nuts
1 6-ounce package semi-
   sweet chocolate bits

Cream butter and sugars. Add beaten eggs. Sift together dry ingredients and add, then add vanilla, nuts and chocolate bits. Drop on ungreased baking sheet. Bake at 375 degrees 10 to 12 minutes. *6 dozen*

Chocolate Nut Drops [FANCY]

Delicate in texture

½ cup butter or margarine
⅔ cup sugar
1 egg, beaten
3 ounces or squares
   unsweetened chocolate,
   melted
2 cups sifted cake flour
½ teaspoon baking soda
½ teaspoon baking powder

¼ teaspoon salt
½ cup milk
1 teaspoon vanilla
½ cup chopped nuts

Cream butter well, adding sugar gradually. Beat until fluffy. Beat in egg. Add cooled chocolate. Sift together dry ingredients and add alternately with milk. Stir in vanilla and nuts. Drop on lightly greased baking sheet. Bake at 350 degrees about 8 minutes. *4 dozen*

Ginger Crinkles [PLAIN]

Made with oil

⅔ cup salad oil	1 teaspoon baking soda
1 cup sugar	1 teaspoon baking powder
1 egg	½ teaspoon salt
4 tablespoons molasses	1 teaspoon cinnamon
2 cups sifted all-purpose	2 teaspoons ginger
flour	¼ cup sugar for dipping

Mix salad oil with sugar. Add egg and beat well. Stir in molasses. Sift together dry ingredients and add. Drop by teaspoonfuls into sugar, then on cookie sheet. Bake at 350 degrees 12 to 15 minutes. *5 dozen*

Molasses Cookies [PLAIN]

Crisply textured

¼ cup shortening	½ teaspoon cloves
½ cup sugar	1 teaspoon ginger
¼ cup molasses	1 teaspoon cinnamon
2 cups sifted all-purpose	½ teaspoon salt
flour	2 tablespoons vinegar
2 teaspoons baking soda	

Melt shortening, sugar and molasses over low heat. Cool. Sift together dry ingredients and add to cooled molasses mixture. Stir in vinegar. Drop on lightly greased baking sheet. Bake at 350 degrees about 8 minutes. *3 dozen*

Oatmeal Crisps [PLAIN]

Crunchy goodness

1 cup sugar	1 teaspoon baking soda
2 cups rolled oats	¾ cup butter
2 cups flour	1 cup raisins
½ teaspoon allspice	1 cup nuts
1 teaspoon cinnamon	2 eggs
1 teaspoon nutmeg	Water
½ teaspoon cloves	

Mix dry ingredients with butter with hands. Add chopped nuts and raisins. Mix into stiff dough with well-beaten eggs and sufficient water to allow dough to be dropped from a spoon. Drop on greased sheet. Bake at 350 degrees 10 to 12 minutes. *About 6 dozen*

Peanut Butter Chocolate Chip Drops [PLAIN]

Good flavors blend

½ cup shortening	1 teaspoon salt
½ cup peanut butter	½ cup milk
1 cup sugar	1 cup rolled oats
2 eggs	1 6-ounce package semi-
1 cup sifted all-purpose	sweet chocolate bits
flour	1 cup chopped nuts
½ teaspoon baking soda	1 teaspoon vanilla
½ teaspoon baking powder	

Blend shortening and peanut butter. Beat in sugar gradually. Add eggs and mix well. Sift together dry ingredients and add alternately with milk. Stir in rolled oats, chocolate pieces, nuts and vanilla. Drop by teaspoonfuls on ungreased baking sheet. Bake at 375 degrees about 12 minutes. *About 5 dozen*

Peanut Crunch Cookies [FANCY]

Special treats

¾ cup butter
1 cup sugar
1 egg
¼ cup milk
1 teaspoon vanilla

2 teaspoons baking powder
½ teaspoon salt
3 cups flour
¾ cup crushed peanut
  brittle

Cream butter and sugar thoroughly. Add egg. Beat well. Add milk and vanilla. Sift together dry ingredients and add. Stir in peanut brittle. Drop on a lightly greased baking sheet. Bake at 375 degrees 10 to 12 minutes. *6 dozen*

Potato Spice Drops [PLAIN]

Old-fashioned flavor

1 cup molasses or honey
½ cup butter or margarine
1 cup cold mashed potatoes
2 cups sifted all-purpose
  flour
½ teaspoon salt
2 teaspoons baking powder

½ teaspoon baking soda
1 teaspoon cinnamon
½ teaspoon allspice
½ teaspoon nutmeg
1 cup seedless raisins
½ cup chopped nuts

Heat molasses or honey and butter until butter melts. Stir in potatoes, blending until smooth. Sift together dry ingredients and add. Stir in raisins and nuts. Drop on greased baking sheet. Bake at 375 degrees 10 to 12 minutes. *4 dozen*

Rye Drops [FANCY]

Deep-fat-fried delicacies

2 eggs, well beaten	1 cup rye flour
2 tablespoons sugar	1 cup white flour
1½ cups sour milk	¼ teaspoon salt
1 teaspoon baking soda	¾ teaspoon cinnamon

Add sugar to beaten eggs and soda to sour milk. Combine. Sift together dry ingredients and add. The dough should be stiff enough to drop off the end of a spoon. Fry in deep fat. Make small so that drops cook in the middle. Roll in powdered sugar and cinnamon before serving. *2½ dozen*

Soft Oatmeal Cookies [PLAIN]

Toddler's delight

½ cup shortening	½ teaspoon salt
1 cup sugar	1 teaspoon cinnamon
2 eggs	½ teaspoon allspice
1½ cups oatmeal	¼ cup milk
1½ cups sifted all-purpose flour	1 teaspoon vanilla
	1 cup seedless raisins
½ teaspoon baking soda	1 cup chopped nuts, if
½ teaspoon baking powder	desired

Cream shortening and sugar. Add eggs and oatmeal. Sift together dry ingredients and add alternately with milk. Add vanilla, raisins and nuts, if used. Drop on lightly greased cookie sheet. Bake at 350 degrees about 12 minutes. *5 dozen*

Sour Cream Crisps [PLAIN]

Buttery good

⅔ cup butter or margarine	2 teaspoons baking powder
1½ cups brown sugar, firmly packed	½ teaspoon baking soda
	¼ teaspoon salt
2 eggs	½ teaspoon cinnamon
1 teaspoon vanilla	¼ teaspoon nutmeg
2½ cups flour	1 cup sour cream

Blend butter, sugar, eggs and flavoring until light and fluffy. Sift together dry ingredients. Add alternately with sour cream to first mixture. Blend well. Drop from teaspoon to greased baking sheet. Bake at 400 degrees 10 to 12 minutes, or until evenly brown. Remove cookies to rack for cooling. *6 dozen*

Sugar and Spice Drops [PLAIN]

Chewy texture

¾ cup butter	¼ teaspoon salt
½ cup brown sugar, firmly packed	½ teaspoon cinnamon
	¼ teaspoon nutmeg
2 eggs	⅛ teaspoon ginger
1¾ cups cake flour	¼ cup milk
1 teaspoon baking powder	¾ cup chopped nuts

Cream butter thoroughly, add sugar gradually, creaming together until light and fluffy. Add eggs one at a time, beating thoroughly after each. Sift together dry ingredients. Add alternately with milk, a small amount at a time, beating after each addition until smooth. Add nuts. Drop from teaspoon on lightly greased baking sheet. Bake at 400 degrees about 10 minutes or until done. *5 dozen*

FILLED COOKIES

Date-filled Drop Cookies [PLAIN]

Quick version

1 cup shortening	3¼ cups sifted all-purpose
2 cups brown sugar, firmly	flour
packed	1 teaspoon salt
2 eggs	1 teaspoon baking powder
⅓ cup milk	Date Nut Filling
1 teaspoon vanilla	

Cream shortening. Add brown sugar gradually, then slightly beaten eggs. Stir in milk and flavoring. Sift together dry ingredients and add. Drop by teaspoonfuls on ungreased baking sheet, leaving room to spread, about 2 inches apart. Center ½ teaspoon of Date Nut Filling on dough, then cover with another ½ teaspoon cookie dough. Bake at 375 degrees about 10 minutes or until lightly browned. *About 5 dozen*

Date Nut Filling:

1½ cups or ½ pound dates,	1 tablespoon lemon juice
pitted and chopped	½ cup chopped nuts
⅔ cup sugar	(optional)
⅔ cup water	

Combine dates, sugar and water. Cook and stir until thick. Remove from heat. Add lemon juice and nuts. Cool before filling cookies.

Georgia's Briars [PLAIN]

Picnic fare

3 cups flour	1 cup lard
1 teaspoon baking soda	¾ cup milk
½ teaspoon salt	

Sift salt and soda with flour into a bowl. Cut in lard. Add milk, stirring to make a ball of dough. Roll a small amount of dough at a time ¼ inch thick. Cut in 3- or 4-inch squares. Place 1 heaping teaspoon of Briars Filling on half of each square. Fold the other half of the square over filling to form a triangle. Press edges together firmly. Bake on lightly greased cookie sheet at 350 degrees 10 to 15 minutes. *About 3 dozen*

Briars Filling:

2 cups raisins	2 cups sugar
2 whole lemons	

Grind raisins in food grinder, using medium knife. Squeeze juice from lemons and pour over ground raisins. Grind lemon rinds in food grinder, using the finest knife. Add with sugar to raisin mixture, stirring thoroughly.

ICEBOX COOKIES

Coconut Wafers [PLAIN]

Memorable goodness

½ cup shortening	½ teaspoon salt
1 cup sugar	1½ teaspoons baking
1 egg	powder
1 teaspoon vanilla	1¾ cups sifted all-purpose
¾ cup fine, flaked coconut	flour

Cream soft shortening and sugar together until light. Beat in egg and vanilla. When well blended, stir in coconut. Sift together dry ingredients and add in three parts, mixing thoroughly. Shape into two long rolls on waxed paper or aluminum foil. Chill 6 to 8 hours. Cut in thin slices. Bake on ungreased sheet at 400 degrees 10 to 12 minutes. *5 dozen*

Nut Thins [PLAIN]

Vary occasionally by using different nuts

½ cup margarine
1 cup brown sugar, firmly packed
1 egg
1 teaspoon vanilla
¼ teaspoon salt

½ teaspoon baking soda
2 cups sifted all-purpose flour
½ cup finely chopped nuts (almonds, filberts, pecans or walnuts)

Cream margarine until soft. Add sugar, then beaten egg and stir to blend well. Add vanilla. Sift together dry ingredients and add half to creamed mixture. Add nuts, then remaining dry ingredients. Shape into two long rolls on waxed paper or aluminum foil. Chill 4 hours. Slice thin. Bake on ungreased cookie sheet at 350 degrees 10 minutes. *5 dozen*

Oatmeal Crisps [PLAIN]

Toasty deliciousness

1 cup shortening
1 cup brown sugar, firmly packed
1 cup white sugar
2 eggs
1½ teaspoons vanilla

1½ cups sifted all-purpose flour
1 teaspoon salt
½ teaspoon baking soda
½ teaspoon baking powder
3 cups quick oats
½ cup finely chopped nuts

Cream shortening until soft, then gradually add sugars, mixing until well blended. Add well-beaten eggs and vanilla. Sift flour with salt, soda and baking powder. Stir into creamed mixture. Add oats and nuts. Divide dough into three portions. Shape into 3-inch rolls on waxed paper or aluminum foil.

Chill 6 to 8 hours. Slice thinly. Bake on ungreased cookie sheets at 375 degrees about 10 minutes. Do not crowd on sheet because there is some spreading. *5 to 6 dozen*

Peanut Butter Crisps [PLAIN]

Nutritious, delicious

½ cup shortening	1 teaspoon vanilla
½ cup peanut butter	1 teaspoon salt
1 cup white sugar	1 teaspoon baking powder
1 cup brown sugar, firmly packed	2 cups sifted all-purpose flour
2 eggs	1½ cups rolled oats

Cream together shortening and peanut butter until well blended. Gradually add sugars. Add beaten eggs and vanilla. Sift together salt, baking powder and flour and stir in gradually, in three portions. Blend in rolled oats, kneading batter with hands, if necessary, until well mixed. Shape dough in rolls on waxed paper or aluminum foil. Chill overnight. Cut slices and bake on lightly greased sheet at 400 degrees 8 to 10 minutes. *4½ dozen*

Spiced Sour Cream Cookies [PLAIN]

Economical and tasty

1 cup shortening	1 teaspoon cinnamon
1¼ cups sugar	½ teaspoon cloves
1 teaspoon vanilla	½ teaspoon nutmeg
2 eggs	3 cups sifted all-purpose flour
1 teaspoon salt	
½ teaspoon baking soda	½ cup thick sour cream
1 teaspoon baking powder	

Cream soft shortening and sugar together until light. Add vanilla and eggs, blending until smooth. Sift together dry ingredients three times, then add alternately with sour cream. Chill 1 hour. Shape chilled dough into long rolls. Wrap in waxed paper or aluminum foil. Chill 6 to 8 hours. Slice thin. Bake on ungreased baking sheet at 400 degrees about 8 to 10 minutes. *About 6 dozen*

Plain Sour Cream Cookies: Follow recipe for Spiced Sour Cream Cookies, using butter in place of shortening and omitting spices. Preparation and baking method are the same.

NO-BAKE COOKIES

Chocolate Crisp Bars [PLAIN]

A-plus for high energy

¼ cup butter or margarine	½ pound fresh marsh-
2 ounces or squares	mallows
unsweetened chocolate	5 cups Puffed Rice

Melt butter, chocolate and marshmallows over very low heat or in top of double boiler. Stir until smooth. Pour marshmallow mixture over Puffed Rice; stir until evenly coated. Spread on greased pan. Let stand until firm. Cut into bars. *3 dozen*

Coconut Fruit Balls [FANCY]

Remember these for Christmas giving

3 cups sugar	2 cups chopped dried apri-
½ tablespoon white corn	cots or pitted dates
syrup	½ cup finely chopped nuts
1 cup rich milk	1 cup flaked coconut
¼ teaspoon salt	

Cook sugar, syrup and milk to soft-ball stage (236 degrees); add fruit and cook 2 minutes more. Remove from heat, cool and knead in nuts. Form into small balls. Roll in flaked coconut. *About 2½ dozen*

Fudgies [PLAIN]

Confectionery dainty

1½ cups rolled oats	¼ cup butter or margarine
1 cup chopped coconut	½ cup brown sugar
1 cup chopped nuts	½ cup white sugar
¼ cup cocoa	½ teaspoon vanilla
¼ cup evaporated milk	

Mix oats, coconut and nuts. Combine cocoa, milk, butter and sugars. Cook over medium heat to full boil. Boil 1 minute, stirring constantly. Remove from heat. Add vanilla. Pour over oats and mix until well coated. Drop on waxed paper. *3 dozen*

Peanut Butter Crispies [PLAIN]

Crunchy golden squares

2 tablespoons butter	½ teaspoon vanilla
2 tablespoons peanut butter	5 cups Rice Krispies
½ pound marshmallows	

Cook butter and peanut butter with marshmallows over boiling water until syrupy, stirring frequently. Add vanilla and beat thoroughly. Put Rice Krispies in a large greased bowl. Pour marshmallow mixture over cereal, stirring briskly. Press into shallow greased pan. When cool, cut into rectangles. *3 dozen*

PRESSED COOKIES

Butterscotch Cookies [PLAIN]

Specially good with pecans

½ cup butter
1 cup brown sugar, firmly
packed
2 eggs
1¼ teaspoons vanilla

½ teaspoon salt
½ teaspoon baking powder
3 cups sifted all-purpose
flour
Chopped pecans for garnish

Cream butter until soft, gradually mixing in sugar. Beat eggs well, then add with flavoring to creamed ingredients. Sift together salt, baking powder and flour and add to butter mixture. Form cookies with a press on an ungreased baking sheet. Garnish with finely chopped pecans, if desired. Bake at 400 degrees 8 to 10 minutes. *About 6 dozen*

ROLLED COOKIES

Chocolate Oatmeal Wafers [PLAIN]

Mint extract adds a flavor surprise

⅔ cup shortening
⅔ cup sugar
1 egg
2 ounces or squares
unsweetened chocolate,
melted

¼ teaspoon vanilla
½ teaspoon mint extract
½ teaspoon salt
1¼ cups sifted all-purpose
flour
¾ cup rolled oats

Blend sugar into soft shortening. Add egg and melted, cooled chocolate, beating well. Stir in flavorings. Sift together salt and flour, then add. Stir in rolled oats. Chill dough 1 hour. Roll thin on lightly floured board. Cut with floured cutters. Bake on lightly greased baking sheet at 350 degrees 8 to 10 minutes. Frost baked, cooled cookies with decorating icing, if desired. *3 to 4 dozen*

Rolled Chocolate Dollars [PLAIN]

A basic rolled dough

2 ounces or squares unsweetened chocolate	2 teaspoons vanilla
1 cup butter or margarine	½ teaspoon salt
⅔ cup sugar	1 teaspoon baking powder
1 egg	3 cups sifted all-purpose flour

Melt and cool chocolate. Cream butter, stir in sugar. Add egg and vanilla. Sift together salt, baking powder and flour. Add cooled chocolate to butter mixture, then sifted dry ingredients. Roll thin, cut and bake on ungreased cookie sheet. Tops may be sprinkled with granulated or colored sugar. Bake at 400 degrees 8 to 10 minutes. Do not overbrown. *About 6 dozen*

Rolled Oatmeal Wafers [PLAIN]

Glaze or decorate these

½ cup butter	¼ teaspoon salt
¾ cup light brown sugar, firmly packed	½ teaspoon baking powder
1 egg	1 cup sifted all-purpose flour
1 teaspoon vanilla	¾ cup rolled oats
2 tablespoons grated orange rind	

Cream butter until soft. Blend in sugar gradually. Add slightly beaten egg and vanilla. Stir in grated orange rind. Sift together salt, baking powder and flour and add to mixture. Stir in rolled oats, mixing well. Chill 1 hour. Roll dough thin on lightly floured board. Cut with floured cutters. Bake on ungreased sheet at 400 degrees 8 to 10 minutes. Cut cookies may be glazed by brushing raw dough with beaten egg white and decorated with candied fruit peel, colored sugar or nut meats. *About 4 dozen*

Spiced Cream Cookies [PLAIN]

Favorite of generations

¾ cup butter or margarine	½ teaspoon cloves
1½ cups sugar	½ teaspoon nutmeg
1¼ teaspoons vanilla	1 teaspoon cinnamon
2 eggs	3½ cups sifted all-purpose
½ teaspoon salt	flour
½ teaspoon baking soda	½ cup sour cream
2 teaspoons baking powder	

Cream butter or margarine until soft, then add sugar, creaming until light. Beat in vanilla and eggs. Sift together salt, soda, baking powder, spices and flour. Add to butter mixture in thirds, alternating with sour cream. Chill, covered, in refrigerator 1 hour or longer. Roll a fourth of dough at a time on very lightly floured board. Cut and place on ungreased sheet. Bake at 375 degrees 10 minutes or until light brown on edge. *6 dozen*

Three R's Mean Cookies Galore

Translated in terms of cookies, the three R's mean cookies that offer a nutritionally worth-while tidbit as well as a goody for the school lunchbox. Cookies that will go to school also should be the keep-fresh kind (for busy mothers may find once a week as often as they'll have time to bake). Nor should they be ones given to shattering or crumbling easily, as is obvious to anyone who has seen the multi-motions to which most lunchboxes are subjected en route to school.

Because cookies are such a popular inclusion in tote lunches, the flavor plus vitamins and minerals are important considerations. Whatever else may be swapped with a friend, count on the cookies being consumed.

Cookies that meet these qualifications include such stay-fresh, non-breakable varieties as Applesauce Gems, Banana, Carrot, Pumpkin and Soft Oatmeal Drops. Honey, Fruit and Mincemeat Bars also measure up to these standards. Soft Molasses Cookies, too, are a worthy addition. For those suggested which are included in other chapters see index.

To keep soft types of cookies soft, store them in an airtight container. If they start to dry, adding a cut piece of apple to the covered cookie jar restores their freshness. Crisp cookies stay at their crunchy best stored loosely covered in a cool, dry place. The oven, once it has cooled, is an excellent place.

STORE THEM RIGHT TO KEEP THEM GOOD

Soft cookies belong in an airtight container to keep that way. Lacking an airtight canister, fruit jars with screw tops work well. Should cookies become hard, they can be restored by adding a slice of apple to the container—but check it for mold and add new piece when necessary.

Crisp cookies should be covered loosely, either in a cookie jar that does not seal tightly or in a container covered loosely with waxed paper. A cold oven is also an excellent storage spot, particularly for meringue and macaroon-type cookies.

To keep supply equal to the cookie demand, many mothers with lunchboxes to fill keep a supply of icebox cookies stored in the refrigerator, ready to bake as needed. This way cookies are always fresh and the cookie-jar raiders cannot so readily deplete those meant to go into the lunchtime kits.

Special occasions call for special desserts and here again cookies will do the trick. For a birthday or a special treat earned by a good report card or service above and beyond the call of duty at home, king-size cookies cut with a coffee-can lid and decorated with the recipient's name in frosting or raisins are popular.

To say "Happy Birthday," cut rolled cookie dough into a candle shape, using a cardboard pattern. Cut around the pattern with a sharp knife. When baked and cooled, decorate the candle with frosting and other festive bits, such as tiny candies, raisins or nuts.

For special holidays, consult the chapter entitled "Decoration Ideas and Frostings." You will find a variety of fancy shapes suggested to suit forthcoming festivities.

So that frosted cookies do not lose their frosting to the wrapping paper, use a frosting that will dry to a hard glaze —Fondant, Decorator's Icing or simple powdered-sugar glazes. Or, if the frosting is primarily for flavoring instead of decorative purposes, make cookies into cookie sandwiches, a most popular move with those who have a real sweet tooth.

No matter which kind of cookies you choose to bake for the lunchbox set, you'll have the satisfaction of knowing that never will there be a more appreciative group of consumers. In the following selection there is a wonderful array of cookies that will cause your youngsters to say, "Boy, Mom, when will you make these again?"

Here is just one of many ways to brighten the day. (See "Decoration Ideas and Frostings" chapter.)

For the birthday child, choose any crisp rolled cookie. Cut the cardboard candle pattern and trace on dough with sharp knife. Bake as recipe directs.

Divide decorative frosting recipe, tinting part yellow for flame and part red for lettering. Candies also can be used for spelling out the greetings.

In this chapter are recipes for these Good Cookies:

PLAIN   FANCY

BALL

Lemon Raisin Treats
Cherry Treats (Variation)
Peanut Butter Cookies
Spiced Butterscotch Balls
Sugar Cookies (Oil)

BARS

Brownies II   *Orange Marmalade*
Chocolate Chip Bars   *Bars I*
Molasses Bars
Raisin Spice Bars

DROP

Applesauce Gems   *Caramel Jumbles*
Butterscotch Drops   *Ranger Cookies*
Chocolate Chip
* Oatmeal Cookies*
Chocolate Drops
Cocoa Nut Cookies
Hermits
Orange Crisps
Prune Drops
Pumpkin Cookies
Raisin Nut Drops
Soft Molasses Cookies
Sour Cream Puffs

PLAIN   FANCY

ICEBOX

Basic Icebox Cookies   *Basic Icebox Cookies*
Plain Variations: *Fancy Variations:*
Butterscotch Slices   *Fruit Slices*
Chocolate Slices   *Nut Slices*
                                          Raisin Spice Slices
                                          Seed Cookies
                                   Date Rounds

NO-BAKE

Marshmallow Chocolate   *Caramel Bars*
Chip Crispies   *Date Crispies*
Peanut Butter Drops

PRESSED

Peanut Butter Press
Cookies

ROLLED

Basic Sugar Cookies
Caramel Cookies
Fruited Bars

Other recipes that could be included in this category are the following (to locate, see index):

BARS
> *Date Bars II*
> *Raisin Oatmeal Bars*

DROP
> *Aladdin Cookies*
> *Applesauce Oatmeal Drops*
> *Buttermilk Cookies, Orange Frosted*
> *Carrot Cookies*
> *Oatmeal Coconut Cherry Crisps*
> *Ragged Robins*

NO-BAKE
> *Fruit Oatmeal Balls*
> *Peanut Butter Crispies*

BALL COOKIES

Lemon Raisin Treats [PLAIN]

High-energy goody

½ cup butter or margarine
¾ cup sugar
1 egg
1 tablespoon lemon juice
Grated rind of ½ lemon
1 teaspoon baking powder
¼ teaspoon salt
1¾ cups sifted all-purpose flour
½ cup raisins (currants, chopped dates or figs may be substituted)

Cream butter with sugar. Blend in egg, lemon juice and grated rind. Sift together dry ingredients and add, mixing until a compact dough is formed. Stir in raisins thoroughly. Form 1-inch balls. Place on lightly greased cookie sheet. Flatten with bottom of glass dipped in flour. Bake at 400 degrees 8 to 10 minutes. *4 dozen*

Cherry Treats [PLAIN]

Prepare dough for Lemon Raisin Treats, substituting ½ teaspoon vanilla and ¼ teaspoon almond extract for lemon juice and grated rind. Add ½ cup chopped, candied red cherries in place of raisins. Form and bake cookies as directed. *4 dozen*

Peanut Butter Cookies [PLAIN]

Crisp favorites

½ cup shortening	2 eggs
½ cup peanut butter	½ teaspoon salt
½ cup white sugar	1 teaspoon baking powder
½ cup brown sugar, firmly packed	½ teaspoon baking soda
½ teaspoon vanilla	1½ cups sifted all-purpose flour

Mix shortening and peanut butter until smoothly blended. Cream in sugars gradually. Stir in vanilla and slightly beaten eggs. Sift together dry ingredients and add to creamed mixture in three portions, mixing thoroughly. Form dough in 1-inch balls. Place on ungreased baking sheet. Press balls down with floured fork so that ridges remain in dough. Bake at 375 degrees 10 minutes or until golden brown. *3 dozen*

Spiced Butterscotch Balls [PLAIN]

These flatten in baking

¼ cup shortening
1½ cups brown sugar
2 tablespoons top milk or
  cream

1 teaspoon cinnamon
1 cup sifted all-purpose
  flour
½ cup chopped nuts

Gradually add sugar to soft shortening. Mix in cream. Add sifted flour and cinnamon. Stir in nuts. Knead dough to compact smoothness. Form in walnut-size balls. Place on greased cookie sheet 3 inches apart, allowing room to spread. Bake at 325 degrees 12 to 15 minutes. *3 dozen*

Sugar Cookies (*Oil*) [PLAIN]

So much faster than the rolled kind and equally good

2½ cups sifted all-purpose
  flour
1 teaspoon baking powder
1 teaspoon salt
½ teaspoon freshly grated
  nutmeg or cinnamon

¾ cup salad oil
1 cup sugar
2 eggs
2 teaspoons vanilla

Sift flour, baking powder, salt and spice together three times. Add sugar to oil in mixing bowl. Beat in eggs one at a time, beating hard after each addition. Add vanilla. Stir in sifted dry ingredients all at once, stirring just to form smooth dough. The dough will be easier to handle if chilled 30 minutes. Shape dough in ½-inch balls. Dip tops in granulated sugar. Place on lightly greased cookie sheet, sugar side up. Flatten balls by pressing lightly with fork tines. Bake at 375 degrees 10 minutes or until lightly browned on edges. *About 5 dozen*

BAR COOKIES

➤ *Brownies II* [PLAIN]

One-bowl method of mixing

½ cup sugar	1 egg
½ cup sifted flour	¼ cup margarine or soft
½ teaspoon baking powder	shortening
¼ teaspoon salt	1 teaspoon vanilla
1 ounce or square	½ cup rolled oats
unsweetened chocolate	½ cup broken nut meats

Sift dry ingredients together into mixing bowl. Melt and cool chocolate. Add chocolate, egg, shortening and vanilla to dry ingredients and beat until smoothly blended. Mix in rolled oats and nut meats. Spread batter in greased 8-inch-square baking pan. Bake at 350 degrees 20 to 25 minutes. Cool on rack. *2 dozen*

➤ *Chocolate Chip Bars* [PLAIN]

Brown-sugar good

1 cup sifted all-purpose flour	½ cup brown sugar, firmly packed
¼ teaspoon salt	1 egg
¼ teaspoon baking soda	½ teaspoon vanilla
½ cup butter or margarine	½ cup semi-sweet chocolate bits

Sift together dry ingredients. Cream butter with brown sugar. Blend in egg and vanilla. Stir in dry ingredients, then chocolate bits. Bake in lightly greased 8 × 12-inch pan at 375 degrees about 15 minutes. Cut into squares while warm. Cool, then remove from pan. *2 dozen*

Molasses Bars [PLAIN]

Old-fashioned favorite

¾ cup brown sugar	¼ teaspoon salt
½ cup butter	¼ teaspoon baking soda
2 eggs	1 teaspoon baking powder
½ cup molasses	1 teaspoon vanilla
1½ cups sifted all-purpose flour	1 cup coarsely chopped nuts

Cream sugar and butter until fluffy. Beat in eggs, one at a time. Blend in molasses. Sift together dry ingredients and add gradually to molasses mixture. Add vanilla and nuts. Bake in greased 9-inch-square pan at 350 degrees about 20 to 25 minutes. Cut into squares while warm. *2 dozen*

Orange Marmalade Bars I [FANCY]

Easy wizardry

2 tablespoons soft butter	1½ cups sifted all-purpose flour
⅔ cup sugar	1 teaspoon baking powder
2 eggs	½ teaspoon salt
⅔ cup orange marmalade	1 cup chopped nuts

Blend butter and sugar. Add eggs and beat well. Add marmalade. Sift together dry ingredients and blend in. Add nuts. Bake in greased 9-inch-square pan at 350 degrees 25 minutes. Cut in squares while warm. *3 dozen*

Raisin Spice Bars [PLAIN]

Ummmm, good

½ cup sugar
¼ cup butter or margarine
1 egg
½ cup molasses
2 cups sifted all-purpose
  flour
½ teaspoon salt

½ teaspoon baking soda
1 teaspoon baking powder
1 teaspoon ginger
1 teaspoon cinnamon
1 teaspoon allspice
½ cup milk
1 cup seedless raisins

Cream butter and sugar. Add egg and molasses. Beat well. Sift together dry ingredients and add alternately with milk. Stir in raisins. Bake in greased 9 × 13-inch pan at 350 degrees 25 to 30 minutes. Cut into bars when cool. *4 dozen*

DROP COOKIES

Applesauce Gems [PLAIN]

Richly moist

1 cup soft shortening
2 cups brown sugar, firmly
  packed
½ cup cold coffee
1 cup applesauce
3½ cups sifted all-purpose
  flour
½ teaspoon baking soda

1 teaspoon baking powder
1 teaspoon salt
1 teaspoon nutmeg
1 teaspoon cinnamon
1 cup light seedless raisins
  or candied diced fruit
1 cup currants or dark
  seedless raisins

Cream shortening and sugar well. Add coffee and applesauce. Sift together dry ingredients and blend in, adding fruits last. Bake on lightly greased baking sheet at 375 degrees about 10 minutes. To keep soft, store in airtight container. *5 dozen*

Butterscotch Drops [PLAIN]

Oil for easy blending

2 eggs
⅔ cup salad oil
1 cup brown sugar, firmly packed
2 cups sifted all-purpose flour

1 teaspoon baking powder
½ teaspoon baking soda
½ teaspoon salt
1 teaspoon cinnamon
1 teaspoon vanilla

Beat eggs well. Add oil and sugar gradually, continuing to beat. Sift together dry ingredients and add. Stir in vanilla. Drop on lightly greased baking sheet. Bake at 400 degrees 8 to 10 minutes. *4 dozen*

Caramel Jumbles [FANCY]

Evaporated-milk-enriched

½ cup soft butter
1 cup brown sugar
½ cup white sugar
2 eggs
1 cup undiluted evaporated milk

1 teaspoon vanilla
2¾ cups flour
½ teaspoon baking soda
½ teaspoon salt
1 cup raisins or chopped dates

Cream butter and sugars well. Beat in eggs. Add evaporated milk and vanilla. Sift together dry ingredients and stir in, then add fruit. Drop on lightly greased baking sheet. Bake at 400 degrees about 10 minutes. When cool, spread with Caramel Jumble Glaze. *3 dozen*

Caramel Jumble Glaze:

2 tablespoons melted butter
¼ cup brown sugar
2 cups sifted powdered
sugar

½ cup undiluted evapo-
rated milk

Stir brown sugar into melted butter until dissolved. Add sugar and milk; beat until fluffy. Spread over cooled cookies.

Chocolate Chip Oatmeal Cookies [PLAIN]

Crunchy-textured

¾ cup butter or margarine
1 cup brown sugar, firmly
packed
½ cup white sugar
2 eggs
1¼ cups sifted all-purpose
flour
1 teaspoon baking powder

¼ teaspoon salt
½ cup milk
3 cups rolled oats
1 6-ounce package semi-
sweet chocolate bits
1 cup chopped nuts
1 teaspoon vanilla

Cream butter and sugars well. Add beaten eggs. Sift together dry ingredients and stir in alternately with milk. Add oats, chocolate bits, nuts and vanilla. Drop on lightly greased baking sheet. Bake at 375 degrees about 12 minutes. *5 dozen*

Chocolate Drops [PLAIN]

Quickly mixed

2 eggs
½ cup salad oil
1 teaspoon vanilla
¾ cup sugar
1¾ cups sifted all-purpose
flour
½ teaspoon baking soda

½ teaspoon baking powder
½ teaspoon salt
2 ounces or squares un-
sweetened chocolate,
melted
½ cup chopped nuts

Beat eggs. Beat in oil and vanilla. Add sugar, mixing well. Sift together dry ingredients and add. Stir in melted, cooled chocolate and nuts. Drop on ungreased cookie sheet. Bake at 375 degrees 8 to 10 minutes. *4 dozen*

Cocoa Nut Cookies [PLAIN]

Coconut added

½ cup butter or margarine	¼ teaspoon salt
1 cup sugar	4 tablespoons cocoa
1 egg	½ cup milk
2 cups sifted all-purpose flour	1 teaspoon vanilla
1 teaspoon baking powder	½ cup chopped nuts
½ teaspoon baking soda	1 cup grated coconut

Cream butter and sugar well. Add beaten egg. Sift together dry ingredients and add alternately with milk. Add vanilla, nuts and coconut. Drop on lightly greased baking sheet. Bake at 350 degrees 10 to 12 minutes. *4 dozen*

Hermits [PLAIN]

Universal favorite

1½ cups brown sugar	1 teaspoon baking powder
¾ cup butter or margarine	1 teaspoon cinnamon
3 eggs	1 teaspoon allspice
½ cup sour milk	½ teaspoon nutmeg
3 cups sifted all-purpose flour	1 cup seedless raisins
½ teaspoon baking soda	½ cup chopped nuts

Cream butter and brown sugar. Add eggs and milk. Sift together dry ingredients and add. Stir in raisins and nuts. Drop on greased baking sheet. Bake at 375 degrees 8 to 10 minutes. *4 dozen*

Orange Crisps [PLAIN]

Very crisp, with delectable orange flavoring

⅔ cup butter
1¼ cups granulated sugar
2 eggs
3 cups sifted all-purpose
  flour

¼ teaspoon salt
2 teaspoons baking powder
Grated rind of 1 orange
1 tablespoon orange juice

Cream shortening with sugar. Beat eggs until light, add and mix well. Sift together flour, salt and baking powder and stir in. Add orange rind and juice. Mix to make smooth dough. Drop by teaspoonfuls onto ungreased cookie sheet. Bake at 325 degrees 12 to 15 minutes. *About 4 dozen*

Prune Drops [PLAIN]

Cinnamon-spiced

⅔ cup shortening
2 cups brown sugar
2 eggs
3½ cups flour
1 teaspoon baking powder
1 teaspoon cinnamon

½ cup milk
1 teaspoon vanilla
½ cup chopped walnuts
½ cup chopped cooked
  prunes

Cream shortening and sugar. Add eggs, beat well. Sift together dry ingredients and add alternately with milk to which vanilla has been added. Stir in nuts and prunes. Drop by spoon onto greased cookie sheet, flattening slightly with spoon or knife. Bake at 350 degrees 10 to 12 minutes. *4 dozen*

Pumpkin Cookies [PLAIN]

Golden goodness

½ cup shortening
½ cup sugar
1 egg
1 cup sifted flour
2 teaspoons baking powder
½ teaspoon salt

1¼ teaspoons cinnamon
⅛ teaspoon ginger
¼ teaspoon nutmeg
½ cup cooked pumpkin
½ cup raisins
½ cup chopped nuts

Cream shortening and sugar together until light. Add unbeaten egg and blend thoroughly. Sift together flour and spices; add to creamed mixture alternately with pumpkin. Add raisins and nuts. Mix well. Drop by teaspoonfuls on greased baking sheet about 2 inches apart, flatten slightly. Bake at 400 degrees about 15 minutes. *2 dozen*

Raisin Nut Drops [PLAIN]

Hearty flavor

¾ cup butter
1 cup sugar
1 cup molasses or corn
   syrup
4 cups sifted flour
1 teaspoon baking soda
1 teaspoon baking powder
1 teaspoon cinnamon

¼ teaspoon cloves
½ teaspoon allspice
1 cup milk
1 cup seedless raisins
1 cup chopped nuts
1 teaspoon grated orange
rind

Cream butter and sugar. Add syrup or molasses. Add sifted dry ingredients alternately with milk. Stir in raisins, nuts and orange rind. Drop on greased cookie sheet. Bake slowly at 350 degrees 12 to 15 minutes. *4½ to 5 dozen*

Ranger Cookies [FANCY]

Satisfying crunchy texture

1 cup shortening	½ teaspoon baking powder
1 cup white sugar	1 teaspoon vanilla
1 cup brown sugar	2 cups quick oatmeal
2 eggs	2 cups Rice Krispies
2 cups flour	1 cup coconut
1 teaspoon baking soda	

Cream shortening and sugars. Add eggs. Sift together dry ingredients and add. Stir in remaining ingredients and drop from teaspoon on baking sheet. Bake at 350 degrees about 12 minutes. *3 dozen*

Soft Molasses Cookies [PLAIN]

Little folks' treat

¼ cup butter or margarine	½ teaspoon baking soda
½ cup brown sugar, firmly packed	½ teaspoon baking powder
	½ teaspoon salt
1 egg	1 teaspoon cinnamon
½ cup molasses	½ teaspoon ginger
2 cups sifted all-purpose flour	½ teaspoon cloves
	½ cup buttermilk

Cream shortening and sugar. Add egg and molasses. Sift together dry ingredients and add alternately with buttermilk. Drop on lightly greased baking sheet. Bake at 375 degrees 8 to 10 minutes. *3 dozen*

Sour Cream Puffs [PLAIN]

Creamy good

½ cup shortening
1 cup brown sugar, firmly packed
1 egg
½ cup seedless raisins
2 cups sifted cake flour

½ teaspoon baking soda
2 teaspoons baking powder
½ teaspoon nutmeg
½ cup commercial sour cream

Cream shortening and sugar. Add beaten egg and raisins. Sift together dry ingredients. Add alternately with sour cream to raisin mixture. Drop by teaspoonfuls on greased cookie sheet. Bake at 350 degrees 12 to 15 minutes. *About 3 dozen*

ICEBOX COOKIES

Basic Icebox Cookies and Variations [PLAIN and FANCY]

All are easy to make

1 cup shortening (part butter for best flavor)
2 cups sugar
2 eggs
1 teaspoon vanilla

½ teaspoon salt
2 teaspoons baking powder
3½ cups sifted all-purpose flour

Cream shortening, gradually add sugar. Beat eggs slightly, add with vanilla to batter, blending smooth. Sift together dry ingredients and stir in, in three portions, working batter well. Shape in 2-inch-diameter rolls. Wrap in waxed paper or aluminum foil. Chill 6 to 8 hours or until firm enough to slice. Cut about ⅛ inch thick. Lay on lightly greased baking sheet. Bake at 400 degrees about 8 to 10 minutes or until lightly browned. *About 7 dozen*

VARIATIONS

Butterscotch Slices: Substitute 2 cups firmly packed brown sugar for white sugar. A more delicate flavor may be obtained with 1 cup brown sugar and 1 cup white sugar.   [PLAIN]

Chocolate Slices: Add 3 squares melted, cooled chocolate to batter after eggs and vanilla are well blended into creamed mixture.   [PLAIN]

Fruit Slices: Add 1 cup finely diced candied fruit such as cherries (red or green or some of each), citron, orange peel or pineapple along with dry ingredients.   [FANCY]

Nut Slices: To dough made with white sugar, brown sugar or chocolate, add 1 to 1½ cups very finely chopped nuts along with sifted dry ingredients.   [FANCY]

Raisin Spice Slices: Add ¼ teaspoon ginger, ½ teaspoon nutmeg, ½ teaspoon allspice and 1 teaspoon cinnamon, sifting together with other dry ingredients. Stir in 1 cup finely chopped raisins.   [FANCY]

Seed Cookies: Add ¼ cup poppy seed or sesame seed to flour mixture and stir into creamed mixture. Strong-flavored seed such as anise or caraway may be added in the proportion of 1 tablespoon to one recipe of basic, plain dough.   [FANCY]

Date Rounds [FANCY]

Winter treat

1 cup shortening	1 cup chopped dates
1 cup white or brown sugar, firmly packed	3½ cups sifted all-purpose flour
1 egg	2 teaspoons baking powder
1 teaspoon vanilla	1½ teaspoons nutmeg
1 teaspoon grated lemon rind	3 tablespoons milk
	1 tablespoon lemon juice

Cream shortening until soft, blend in sugar. Add slightly beaten egg, vanilla, grated lemon rind and dates. Sift together dry ingredients and add alternately with milk and lemon juice. Form in long rolls. Wrap in waxed paper or aluminum foil. Chill overnight. Bake ¼-inch-thick slices on slightly greased baking sheet at 400 degrees 10 to 12 minutes. *5 dozen*

NO-BAKE COOKIES

Caramel Bars [FANCY]

Rich with nuts

1½ cups Puffed Rice or Wheat	¼ cup evaporated milk
	¼ cup butter or margarine
1 cup chopped coconut	1 cup brown sugar
1 cup chopped nuts	½ teaspoon vanilla

Mix cereal, coconut and nuts. Combine evaporated milk, butter and sugar and cook over medium heat to full boil. Boil 1 minute, stirring constantly. Remove from heat. Add vanilla. Pour over cereal mixture. Stir until coated evenly. Spread in buttered 9 × 13-inch pan. Let stand until firm. Cut into squares. *3 dozen*

Date Crispies [FANCY]

Deliciously fruited

¼ cup butter	5 cups Rice Krispies
½ pound marshmallows	1 cup chopped dates
¼ teaspoon vanilla	

Cook butter and marshmallows over boiling water until syrupy, stirring frequently. Add vanilla and beat thoroughly.

Put Rice Krispies in large greased bowl. Add dates and mix. Pour on marshmallow mixture, stirring briskly. Press into shallow, greased pan. Cut into squares when cool. *3 dozen*

Marshmallow Chocolate Chip Crispies [PLAIN]

Youngsters can make these

6 tablespoons butter
½ pound marshmallows
1 cup semi-sweet chocolate
  bits

½ teaspoon vanilla
3½ cups Rice Krispies or
  cornflakes

Melt butter and marshmallows in double boiler, then stir in chocolate bits. Blend well. Remove from heat. Add vanilla. Butter large bowl, pour in Rice Krispies. Pour chocolate mixture over cereal. Stir well. Pat into a shallow buttered 9 × 12-inch pan. When cool, cut into bars. *4 dozen 1 × 2-inch bars*

Peanut Butter Drops [PLAIN]

Oats for energy

2 cups sugar
½ cup butter
½ cup milk
3 cups quick oats

5 tablespoons peanut butter
½ cup chopped nuts
1 teaspoon vanilla

Boil together sugar, butter and milk 1 minute. Pour while hot over oats and peanut butter. Add nuts and vanilla. Mix quickly. Drop by spoonfuls on waxed paper. Let stand until firm. *3 dozen*

PRESSED COOKIES

Peanut Butter Press Cookies [PLAIN]
New dress for an old favorite

½ cup shortening
½ cup peanut butter
½ cup white sugar
½ cup brown sugar
1 egg
1 teaspoon vanilla

2 teaspoons milk
¼ teaspoon baking soda
¼ teaspoon baking powder
1¼ cups sifted all-purpose
flour

Cream shortening and peanut butter together. Blend in sugars gradually until smooth. Add slightly beaten egg, vanilla and milk. Sift together dry ingredients and stir in gradually. Form cookies with press on an ungreased baking sheet. Bake until golden brown at 375 degrees about 10 to 12 minutes. *3½ dozen*

ROLLED COOKIES

Basic Sugar Cookies [PLAIN]
Always welcomed

½ cup butter
1 cup sugar
1 egg
1 teaspoon vanilla

½ teaspoon baking powder
¼ teaspoon salt
2 cups sifted all-purpose
flour

Cream butter, blend in sugar. Add egg and vanilla or other desired flavoring. Sift together dry ingredients and stir in. Chill dough 1 hour. Roll thin on lightly floured board. Cut into shapes with cookie cutter, pastry wheel or sharp knife. Bake on ungreased sheet at 400 degrees 8 minutes. *4 dozen*

Caramel Cookies [PLAIN]

Roll thin for crispness

½ cup butter or margarine
1 cup brown sugar, firmly
  packed
1 egg
1 teaspoon vanilla

2 teaspoons baking powder
½ teaspoon salt
2 cups sifted all-purpose
  flour

Cream butter, add sugar gradually. Add egg and vanilla, beating in well. Sift together dry ingredients and add. Roll thin on lightly floured board. Cut into fancy shapes or with small round cutter. Bake on ungreased sheet at 400 degrees 8 to 10 minutes. *4 dozen*

Fruited Bars [PLAIN]

Chewy goodness

½ cup shortening
¾ cup white sugar or
  firmly packed brown sugar
1 egg
2 teaspoons lemon juice
¼ teaspoon salt
1 teaspoon baking powder
1 teaspoon cinnamon

½ teaspoon cloves
½ teaspoon nutmeg
1¾ cups sifted all-purpose
  flour
2 tablespoons sweet or sour
  milk
½ cup ground raisins
¼ cup currants

Cream shortening until soft, stir in sugar well. Add slightly beaten egg and lemon juice. Sift together dry ingredients and blend into mixture alternately with milk. Add fruits. (Chopped dates or candied fruits may be substituted for raisins and currants.) Roll out on floured board. Cut in small bars. Bake on lightly greased sheet at 400 degrees 8 to 10 minutes. *4 dozen*

Four Score or More

Some occasions call for cookies in more than usual numbers—holiday seasons, teas, wedding receptions, club and church gatherings. At times like these it is practical to start with a recipe that turns out cookies in large numbers so that time spent measuring and mixing is kept to a minimum. You'll find a tempting array from which to choose in the following collection.

The Butter Crisps and the Rolled Cookies to Decorate both lend themselves well to varying in many ways. Divide the one big batch into perhaps six or seven smaller batches to color, flavor, shape and decorate so that each baking has its own personality and only you are wise to the fact that they all began as one basic dough. You'll find specific suggestions on how to vary and trim cookies in the chapter entitled "Decoration Ideas and Frostings."

Though not quite so versatile because they have a more distinctive flavor of their own, the Caramel Cookies and Molasses Drops can be varied by adding nuts, coconut, dates or other dried fruits, or by frosting them with any icing that uses these.

The cookie mixes you may make and bake all at once, varying them according to the recipes given with each of the basic-mix recipes—or you may store the mix on your kitchen shelf to bake as needed. Here again, one mixing produces a vast number of cookies, a time and labor saving indeed worth while. Dry mixes should be kept absolutely airtight in a cool, dry place. Stored this way, they keep well 2 to 3 months.

In this chapter are recipes for these Good Cookies:

PLAIN   FANCY

DROP

Raisin Drop Cookies

ICEBOX

Butter Crisps

PRESSED OR DROP

Caramel Cookies

ROLLED

Molasses Drops
Rolled Cookies to
    Decorate
        Chocolate Variation

QUANTITY MIXES

Basic Cookie Mix
    Plain Cookies Made from
    Basic Cookie Mix:
        Ginger Cookies
        Peanut Butter
            Cookies

Basic Cookie Mix
    Fancy Cookies Made
    from Basic Cookie
    Mix:
        Banana Coconut Drops
        Cocoa Raisin Drops

Oatmeal Cookie Mix
    Plain Cookies Made from
    Oatmeal Cookie Mix:
        Chocolate Chippers
        Peanut Butter Drops
        Raisin Drops

Oatmeal Cookie Mix
    Fancy Cookies Made
    from Oatmeal Cookie
    Mix:
        Gumdrop Chews
        Tropical Drops

DROP COOKIES

Raisin Drop Cookies [FANCY]

Quantity recipe

6 cups seedless raisins
2 pounds butter or
  margarine
2 pounds sugar (4 cups)
1 pint honey (2 cups)
8 eggs, beaten
1 cup milk
2 pounds sifted flour
  (8 cups)

2 tablespoons baking
  powder
1 tablespoon salt
1 tablespoon cinnamon
1 tablespoon nutmeg
3 cups grated coconut
1 box (1⅓ pounds) corn-
  flakes

Pour boiling water over raisins and let stand 5 minutes. Drain. Cream butter and sugar well. Beat in honey, eggs and milk. Sift together dry ingredients and add. Add raisins, coconut and cornflakes, blending thoroughly but gently. Drop on lightly greased baking sheets. Bake at 375 degrees 12 to 15 minutes. *200 cookies*

ICEBOX COOKIES

Butter Crisps [PLAIN]

Quantity recipe

2 cups butter
2 cups sugar
4 eggs
2 teaspoons vanilla

2 teaspoons almond extract
¼ teaspoon salt
5 cups sifted all-purpose
  flour

Cream butter and sugar thoroughly. Add eggs and beat until light and fluffy. Add flavorings, salt and flour. Mix until dough is formed. Shape into long rolls, 1 to 1½ inches in diameter, or into long oblong bars. Wrap in waxed paper and chill until firm. When ready to bake, slice thin and bake on ungreased baking sheets at 400 degrees 8 to 10 minutes. *12 dozen*

NOTE: Raw dough may be frozen after wrapping bars in freezer packaging.

PRESSED OR DROP COOKIES

Caramel Cookies [PLAIN]

Quantity recipe

1 cup shortening	1 teaspoon salt
½ cup brown sugar	½ teaspoon baking soda
1 cup white sugar	5 cups sifted all-purpose
3 eggs	flour
2 teaspoons vanilla	

Cream shortening. Blend in sugars gradually, beating well. Add eggs and vanilla. Sift together dry ingredients and add gradually. Shape through cookie press or drop by spoonfuls onto ungreased baking sheet. Bake at 375 degrees 8 to 10 minutes. *9 dozen*

[1] At left on rack, *Chocolate Chip Cookies* decorated with *Chocolate Dip,*
drizzled on with tip of spoon; in center, *Caramel Cookies, Chocolate Dip*
filled. Round rack shows more *Chocolate Chip Cookies.* Rack at right holds
Bourbon Balls, some rolled in powdered sugar, others left plain. Rack left,
on board, are *Chocolate Chip Dream Bars* topped with *Orange Frosting*
and *Chocolate Dip;* and *Chocolate Chip Bars* with white *Fondant Frosting*
and chocolate chips.

Color plate courtesy of The Nestlé Co.

[2] Encircling punch bowl and in foreground are *Molasses Dolls* cut and decorated in a variety of ways. In fluted paper cups are *Almond-Filled Tarts* baked in fluted pans lined with the baking cups. In old-fashioned wooden bun basket are *Butter Nut Balls*.

Color plate courtesy of the American Dairy Association

ROLLED COOKIES

Molasses Drops [PLAIN]

Quantity recipe

1 cup shortening	1 teaspoon baking powder
1 cup brown sugar	1 teaspoon baking soda
1 egg	3 teaspoons cinnamon
1 cup molasses	3 teaspoons ginger
5 cups sifted all-purpose flour	

Cream shortening and sugar well. Add egg and molasses. Sift together dry ingredients and add. Chill about 1 hour, then roll on board dusted with mixture of equal parts flour and granulated sugar, rolling only a small amount of dough at a time. Bake on lightly greased sheet at 375 degrees 8 to 10 minutes. *10 dozen*

Rolled Cookies to Decorate [PLAIN]

Quantity recipe

2 cups butter or margarine	5 cups sifted all-purpose flour
3 cups sugar	
4 eggs	1 teaspoon baking powder
¼ cup milk	1 teaspoon salt
4 teaspoons vanilla	

Cream butter well. Beat in sugar gradually. Add eggs, milk and vanilla and blend well. Sift together dry ingredients, add and blend well. Chill 2 hours. Roll and cut as desired. Bake on ungreased baking sheet at 375 degrees 8 to 10 minutes. *15 dozen*

Chocolate Variation: To half of dough, add 2 ounces or squares melted, cooled unsweetened chocolate, adding with eggs.

VARIATION OF ROLLED COOKIES

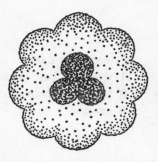 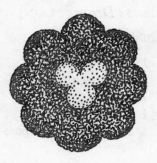

"Mosaic" cookies—cut from two contrasting rolled doughs—one dark or tinted and one light.

Light dough base cookie. Remove center with small fancy cutter. Insert center cut out of dark dough before baking.

Dark dough base cookie. Remove center with small fancy cutter. Insert center cut out of light dough before baking.

QUANTITY MIXES

Basic Cookie Mix

Quantity recipe

6 cups sifted all-purpose flour	2 teaspoons salt
1 cup sifted non-fat dry milk	2 cups granulated sugar
6 teaspoons baking powder	1½ cups shortening or margarine

Sift together dry ingredients. Cut in shortening with two knives or pastry blender until in fine particles. Store in airtight container at room temperature. Mix will keep on shelf for two to three months if stored in cool, dry place, tightly covered. *10 cups mix*

Banana Coconut Drops [FANCY]

Party fare

2 cups Basic Cookie Mix, firmly packed
1 medium banana, mashed
½ cup grated coconut
½ cup chopped nuts
1 egg, beaten
1 teaspoon vanilla

Combine all ingredients in bowl and blend with fork until dough is formed. Drop on lightly greased baking sheet. Bake at 375 degrees 10 to 12 minutes. *2½ dozen*

Cocoa Raisin Drops [FANCY]

Lunchtime treat

2 cups Basic Cookie Mix, firmly packed
¼ cup powdered cocoa
¼ cup sugar
1 teaspoon vanilla
½ cup raisins
2½ tablespoons water

Combine all ingredients in bowl. Mix gently just until dry mix is moistened. Drop on lightly greased baking sheet. Bake at 350 degrees 10 to 12 minutes. *2½ dozen*

Ginger Cookies [PLAIN]

Sugar-crested

2 cups Basic Cookie Mix, firmly packed
½ teaspoon each ginger, cinnamon and allspice
½ teaspoon vanilla
4 tablespoons molasses
1 egg, beaten

Combine all ingredients in bowl. Stir just until blended. Drop by teaspoonfuls on lightly greased baking sheet. Flatten with bottom of glass dipped in granulated sugar. Bake at 375 degrees about 8 minutes. *2 dozen*

Peanut Butter Cookies [PLAIN]

Good any time

2 cups Basic Cookie Mix, firmly packed

2 tablespoons cold coffee

3 tablespoons peanut butter

1 tablespoon honey or molasses

1 teaspoon vanilla

Combine all ingredients, blending well with fork. Shape into balls the size of marbles. Press down on ungreased baking sheet, crisscrossing with tines of fork. Bake at 375 degrees about 10 minutes. *2½ dozen*

Oatmeal Cookie Mix

Quantity recipe

4 cups sifted flour

2 teaspoons baking powder

2 teaspoons baking soda

2 teaspoons salt

1 cup brown sugar

1 cup granulated sugar

2 cups shortening

4 cups uncooked rolled oats

Sift together flour, baking powder, soda and salt. Mix in sugars. Cut in shortening until mixture resembles fine crumbs. Add rolled oats, mixing well. Store at room temperature in tightly covered container. *12 cups mix*

Chocolate Chippers [PLAIN]

Children's delight

2 cups Oatmeal Cookie Mix

¼ cup undiluted evaporated milk

1 cup chocolate bits

½ cup chopped nuts

Combine all ingredients thoroughly. Drop on lightly greased baking sheet. Bake at 375 degrees 10 to 12 minutes. *2 dozen*

Gumdrop Chews [FANCY]

Quickly made

2 cups Oatmeal Cookie Mix	1 egg, beaten
	½ cup sliced gumdrops
2 tablespoons milk	½ cup grated coconut

Mix all ingredients well. Drop on lightly greased baking sheet. Bake at 375 degrees 12 to 15 minutes. *2 dozen*

Peanut Butter Drops [PLAIN]

Delightfully crunchy

2 cups Oatmeal Cookie Mix	½ cup peanut butter
	½ teaspoon vanilla
¼ cup honey	½ cup chopped nuts

Blend ingredients well. Drop on lightly greased baking sheet. Bake at 375 degrees 12 to 15 minutes. *2 dozen*

Raisin Drops [PLAIN]

Reliable goodness

2 cups Oatmeal Cookie Mix	½ teaspoon vanilla
	½ cup seedless raisins
2 tablespoons milk	½ cup chopped nuts
1 egg	

Combine all ingredients and blend well. Drop on lightly greased baking sheet. Bake at 375 degrees 12 to 15 minutes. *2 dozen*

Tropical Drops [FANCY]

Richly fruited

3 cups Oatmeal Cookie Mix	¼ cup chopped maraschino cherries
½ cup mashed banana	¼ cup grated coconut
¼ cup crushed pineapple, drained	

Combine all ingredients well. Drop on lightly greased baking sheet. Bake at 375 degrees 12 to 15 minutes. *3 dozen*

To Mail with Love

Cookies mean a bit of home to those away from it—and who doesn't enjoy dipping his hand into a cookie jar now and then? First in importance is the right cookie for keeping qualities. Next consider packaging. Then, in shipping, use the method that insures the greatest speed. Air mail—often the most satisfactory, and sometimes the only way for servicemen —*is* expensive. Be sure your cookies are worth the effort and cost.

Cookies that arrive a jumble of crumbs or off-flavor mean only disappointment to the receiver. The right cookie for shipping is one of exceptional keeping qualities. Fruit bars, applesauce drops and honey cookies and shortbread are among the more successful travelers in the cookie world. But even these can be damaged beyond edibility if proper care in packaging is not exercised.

Choose a container that will not be crushed. Corrugated paper liners overlaid with foil or waxed paper inside a metal tin are a good beginning. Failing a tin, choose a box with stiff, rigid sides and line it with a covering of corrugated paper. Make even layers of individually waxed-paper-wrapped cookies or fill spaces with crumpled paper or popcorn so that cookies do not slip and slide about. Overwrap the container with additional corrugated paper, sturdy outside wrapping paper and a heavy twine, securely knotted. Have the post office stamp the package "Perishable."

STEPS TO SUCCESSFUL MAILING

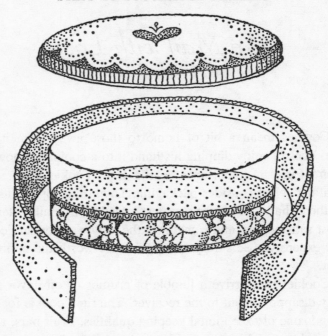

Select a "good traveler" from recipes in this chapter and read over-all instructions at beginning of chapter carefully. Use metal container or sturdy box.

Wrap cookies individually, preferably in moisture-vaporproof paper. Fill in any air spaces with popcorn or crumpled paper. Protect each layer with corrugated paper liner.

Overwrap container with corrugated paper before wrapping in sturdy outside paper. Mail by quickest means available and have post office mark package "Perishable."

A word about decoration of cookies: nuts that may go rancid, chocolate that may discolor from excessive heat, and decorating frostings that are apt to become either sticky or stale should be avoided. This is particularly true when the cookie will be eaten perhaps two to three weeks after baking day.

There are, however, a number of cookies that are sophisticated travelers when prepared, packed and shipped with care. Choose one of these to mail with love and peace of mind.

In this chapter are recipes for these Good Cookies:

PLAIN   FANCY

BALL

Grandma's Nutlets
Honey Peanut Butter Balls

BARS

Date Bars II   *Gumdrop Squares*
Fruit Bars
Honey Bars
Mincemeat Bars
Raisin Oatmeal Bars

DROP

Applesauce Oatmeal Drops
Carrot Cookies
Date Drops
Ginger Softies
Gumdrop Jewels
Honey Drops
Mincemeat Drops
Oatmeal Sesame Chews
Rocks

PLAIN   FANCY

ICEBOX

Ginger Slices
Honey Icebox Cookies
Molasses Rounds

NO-BAKE

No-bake Fruit Oatmeal Balls

Other recipes that could be included in this category are the following (to locate, see index):

BALL
    Date Bowlers
    Ginger Mounds
BARS
    Chinese Chews
    Date Bars I
    Orange Marmalade Bars I
DROP
    Fruit Drops
    Date Surprises
    Soft Oatmeal Drops
FILLED
    Phoebe's Fig-filled Cookies
ROLLED
    Fruited Bars

BALL COOKIES

Grandma's Nutlets [PLAIN]

Delightfully flavored with honey, brown sugar and cinnamon

1 cup shortening	4 cups sifted all-purpose
1 cup brown sugar	flour
1 egg	2 teaspoons baking soda
1 cup honey	1 teaspoon salt
1 cup finely chopped nuts (omit for distant mailing)	1 teaspoon cinnamon

Cream shortening and brown sugar together. Add egg, honey and nuts. Sift together dry ingredients and add in three portions to mixture. Form in small balls. Bake on lightly greased sheet at 325 degrees about 15 minutes or until lightly browned. *About 7 dozen*

Honey Peanut Butter Balls [PLAIN]

Crisp bites that melt in your mouth

½ cup shortening	1 egg
½ cup peanut butter	2 cups sifted all-purpose
½ cup honey	flour
½ cup brown sugar, firmly packed	½ teaspoon salt
	½ teaspoon baking soda

Cream shortening and peanut butter together. Blend in honey and sugar until fluffy. Stir in well-beaten egg. Sift together dry ingredients and add, mixing well. Form small balls. Place on lightly greased sheet. Press down with fork. Bake at 350 degrees 8 to 10 minutes. *4 dozen*

BAR COOKIES

Date Bars II [PLAIN]

Stay moist and chewy

3 eggs, beaten
1 cup sugar
1 teaspoon vanilla
3 tablespoons flour (yes,
  that's right)
½ teaspoon baking powder

¼ teaspoon salt
1 cup finely chopped dates
1 cup chopped nuts (omit
  if mailing cookies far
  away)

Combine eggs, sugar and vanilla, beating well. Sift dry ingredients over dates and nuts, then add. Bake in greased 9-inch-square pan at 325 degrees about 35 minutes. Cut into squares while warm, dusting with powdered sugar, if desired. *2 dozen*

Fruit Bars [PLAIN]

Like Grandma's—chewy and delicious

1 cup seedless raisins
½ cup water
½ cup shortening
1 cup sugar
2 eggs
2 cups sifted all-purpose
  flour

1 teaspoon baking powder
1 teaspoon cinnamon
¼ teaspoon nutmeg
1 teaspoon vanilla
½ cup finely broken nuts, if
  desired

Boil raisins in water 5 minutes. Cool to lukewarm. Cream shortening and sugar. Beat in eggs one at a time. Add cooled raisins. Sift together dry ingredients and add with vanilla and nuts. Bake in greased 9 × 13-inch pan at 375 degrees about 15 minutes. Cool, then cut into squares or oblongs. *About 3 dozen*

Gumdrop Squares [FANCY]

Gay 'n' chewy with slices of gumdrops

3 eggs, separated
¼ teaspoon cream of tartar
½ cup brown sugar, firmly packed
¼ teaspoon baking soda
¼ teaspoon salt
⅓ cup sifted all-purpose flour

1 tablespoon melted butter
¼ teaspoon vanilla
1 cup sliced gumdrops (no licorice)
½ cup chopped nuts, if desired

Beat egg whites until stiff with cream of tartar. Beat egg yolks until thick and lemon-colored, gradually beating in brown sugar. Sift soda and salt with flour. Fold into yolk mixture. Add butter and vanilla. Fold in stiffly beaten egg whites. Spread in greased 9 × 13-inch pan. Sprinkle with nuts and gumdrops. Bake at 375 degrees about 15 minutes. Cut into squares while warm. *About 3 dozen*

Honey Bars [PLAIN]

Graham cracker crumbs make these crunchingly good

1 cup chopped dates or figs
1 cup chopped nuts (omit if mailing a long distance)
2 eggs
¾ cup honey

½ cup sifted all-purpose flour
½ cup finely crushed graham cracker crumbs
¼ teaspoon salt

Combine dates and nuts. Beat eggs till light, gradually adding honey and continuing to beat. Fold in sifted flour. Add cracker crumbs, then dates, nuts and salt. Bake in greased 8-inch-square pan at 350 degrees about 35 minutes. Cut into squares while warm. *2 dozen*

➤ *Mincemeat Bars* [PLAIN]

Spicy with cakelike texture

⅓ cup shortening
1 cup brown sugar
2 eggs
1 cup mincemeat
½ cup chopped nuts
  (optional)

2 cups sifted all-purpose
  flour
½ teaspoon baking soda
1 teaspoon baking powder

Cream shortening and sugar. Beat eggs, add and mix well. Stir in mincemeat and nuts. Sift together dry ingredients and add. Spread in greased 9 × 13-inch pan. Bake at 350 degrees 30 minutes. Cut into squares while still warm. *3 dozen*

Raisin Oatmeal Bars [PLAIN]

Flavored with orange juice and rind

1¼ cups brown sugar
⅓ cup butter or margarine,
  melted
2 eggs
1 cup sifted all-purpose
  flour
½ teaspoon salt
½ teaspoon baking powder

½ cup rolled oats
¼ cup orange juice
1 teaspoon grated orange
  rind
1 cup seedless raisins
½ cup chopped nuts
  (optional)

Blend brown sugar and butter well. Add eggs one at a time. Sift flour, salt and baking powder. Add with oats, orange juice and rind. Add raisins and nuts. Spread in greased 9-inch-square pan. Bake at 375 degrees about 20 minutes. Cut into squares while warm. *3 dozen*

DROP COOKIES

Applesauce Oatmeal Drops [PLAIN]

Low in fat, sugar and *calories!*

¼ cup butter or margarine
¼ cup brown sugar
¼ cup white sugar
½ cup applesauce
1 cup sifted all-purpose
   flour

½ teaspoon baking soda
1 teaspoon baking powder
½ teaspoon salt
1 cup rolled oats
½ cup seedless raisins

Cream butter and sugars. Add applesauce. Sift together dry ingredients and stir in. Add oats and raisins. Drop by spoonfuls onto lightly greased cookie sheet. Bake at 375 degrees about 10 minutes. *3 dozen*

Carrot Cookies [PLAIN]

Different and delicious

½ cup butter or margarine
1 cup brown sugar
½ cup white sugar
2 eggs
2 cups sifted all-purpose
   flour
2 teaspoons baking powder
½ teaspoon baking soda

½ teaspoon salt
1 teaspoon cinnamon
½ teaspoon nutmeg
2 cups rolled oats
1 cup raisins
1 cup grated raw carrots
1 cup chopped nuts (omit
   if mailing far away)

Cream shortening and sugars well. Add beaten eggs. Sift together dry ingredients and stir in. Add raisins, carrots and nuts. Drop onto lightly greased baking sheet. Flatten slightly. Bake at 350 degrees 25 to 30 minutes. *3 dozen*

Date Drops [PLAIN]

Rich-flavored 'n' chewy

2 cups finely chopped dates	½ teaspoon baking soda
1 cup water	1 teaspoon baking powder
1½ cups white sugar	1 teaspoon salt
1 cup brown sugar	1 cup chopped nuts (omit
1 cup butter or margarine	if mailing far away)
3 eggs, beaten	
1 teaspoon vanilla	
4 cups sifted all-purpose flour	

Cook dates with ½ cup of the white sugar and the water until thick. Cool. Cream butter and remaining sugar. Add eggs and vanilla. Sift together dry ingredients and add. Stir in nuts and cooled date mixture. Drop on greased cookie sheet. Bake at 375 degrees 12 to 15 minutes. *5 dozen*

Ginger Softies [PLAIN]

Soft, sweet and spicy—makes a big batch

1 cup butter or margarine	1½ teaspoons cinnamon
1 cup sugar	½ teaspoon allspice
1 egg	2 teaspoons baking soda
2 cups molasses	2 teaspoons baking powder
2 tablespoons vinegar	1 teaspoon salt
1 cup boiling water	
7 cups sifted flour	
2 tablespoons ginger	

Cream butter and sugar. Add egg, molasses, vinegar and boiling water. Sift together dry ingredients and add, stirring just to blend. Drop onto lightly greased baking sheet. Sprinkle with sugar. Bake at 350 degrees 8 to 10 minutes. *8 dozen*

Gumdrop Jewels [PLAIN]

1 cup shortening
1 cup brown sugar, firmly packed
1 egg
1 teaspoon vanilla
1 cup sifted all-purpose flour
½ teaspoon baking powder
½ teaspoon baking soda
½ teaspoon salt
½ cup chopped nuts (omit if mailing far away)
1 cup quick oats
½ cup gumdrops, cut up
½ cup diced, candied fruit

Cream shortening and sugar. Add egg and vanilla. Sift together dry ingredients and add. Stir in nuts, oats and gumdrops. Drop on greased baking sheet. Bake at 350 degrees 10 to 12 minutes. *3 dozen*

Honey Drops [PLAIN]

Stay soft and nicely moist

⅓ cup melted butter or margarine
1 cup honey
2 eggs
½ cup milk
3½ cups sifted all-purpose flour
2 teaspoons baking powder
½ teaspoon baking soda
1 teaspoon cinnamon
½ teaspoon allspice
1 cup raisins or chopped figs
1 cup chopped nuts (omit if sending far away)

Add melted butter to honey. Stir in eggs and milk. Sift together dry ingredients and add. Stir in fruit and nuts. Bake at 375 degrees 12 to 15 minutes. *4 dozen*

Mincemeat Drops [PLAIN]

Spicy-and-chewy good

1 cup shortening
1½ cups sugar
3 eggs
3¼ cups sifted all-purpose
flour
½ teaspoon salt

½ teaspoon baking soda
1 teaspoon baking powder
1¼ cups prepared mince-
meat
1 cup chopped nuts (omit
if mailing far away)

Cream shortening and sugar. Beat eggs and add, then sift together dry ingredients and add. Stir in mincemeat. Add nuts and drop onto lightly greased baking sheet. Bake at 375 degrees 10 to 12 minutes. *4 dozen*

Oatmeal Sesame Chews [PLAIN]

Intriguing flavor—not too sweet

2 cups rolled oats
2½ cups boiling water
1 teaspoon salt
½ cup sugar

½ cup shortening
½ cup grated coconut
Sesame seed
Brown sugar

Cook oats in boiling, salted water 3 minutes. Add sugar and shortening. Let melt in hot cereal. Add coconut. Coat top of each drop cookie in mixture of sesame seed and brown sugar before placing on greased cookie sheet. Bake at 350 degrees 12 to 15 minutes. *4 dozen*

Rocks [PLAIN]

Deliciously fruited mounds

½ cup butter or margarine
½ cup brown sugar
½ cup white sugar
2 eggs, well beaten
2 cups flour
½ teaspoon baking powder
1 cup chopped dates, figs or
   raisins

½ cup chopped nuts (omit
   if mailing far away)
1 teaspoon vanilla
½ teaspoon baking soda
2 teaspoons hot water

Cream butter and sugars. Add eggs. Sift flour and baking powder. Add with dates, nuts and vanilla. Dissolve soda in hot water and stir in. Drop onto lightly greased baking sheet. Bake at 350 degrees 10 to 12 minutes. *4 dozen*

ICEBOX COOKIES

Ginger Slices [PLAIN]

Crisp, spicy—with no eggs

1 cup shortening
1 cup brown sugar
1 cup dark corn syrup
1 cup chopped nuts (omit if
   mailing far away)
4½ cups sifted all-purpose
   flour

1 teaspoon salt
1½ teaspoons baking
   powder
1½ teaspoons ginger
1 teaspoon cinnamon
3 tablespoons milk

Cream soft shortening with sugar. Add corn syrup, then finely chopped nuts. Sift together dry ingredients. Add half to shortening mixture. Add milk, then remaining flour mixture.

Shape into two rolls on waxed paper or aluminum foil. Chill overnight or at least 6 hours. Cut in thin slices. Bake on lightly greased cookie sheet at 375 degrees 10 to 12 minutes. Do not overbrown or cookies will be hard. *About 6 to 7 dozen*

Honey Icebox Cookies [PLAIN]

Laced with nuts and spice

2½ cups sifted all-purpose flour	1 egg
2 teaspoons baking powder	½ cup sugar
½ teaspoon salt	½ teaspoon vanilla
½ teaspoon cinnamon	½ cup honey
½ cup finely chopped nuts (omit if mailing far away)	¾ cup melted butter or margarine

Sift together flour, baking powder, salt and cinnamon three times, the last time into bowl. Stir in nuts. Beat egg well. Add remaining ingredients to egg. Stir into dry ingredients, blending well. Chill thoroughly, about 2 hours. Shape into rolls and wrap in waxed paper or aluminum foil. Chill overnight. Slice thin. Bake on ungreased sheet at 400 degrees 8 to 10 minutes. *4 dozen*

Molasses Rounds [PLAIN]

Less sweet, with rich molasses 'n' spice flavor

1 cup shortening	½ teaspoon baking soda
½ cup brown sugar, firmly packed	1 teaspoon salt
⅓ cup molasses	½ teaspoon ginger
1 egg	1 teaspoon cinnamon
2 teaspoons vinegar	¼ teaspoon nutmeg
3 cups sifted all-purpose flour	¼ teaspoon cloves

Add brown sugar to soft shortening. Stir in molasses, egg and vinegar; beat until blended. Sift together dry ingredients and add in three portions to shortening mixture, blending smooth after each addition. Chill dough 2 hours. Divide dough into three portions. Shape each into a long roll. Wrap in waxed paper or aluminum foil. Chill overnight. Slice thin and bake on ungreased cookie sheet at 350 degrees 10 minutes. *7 dozen*

NO-BAKE COOKIES

No-bake Fruit Oatmeal Balls [FANCY]

Delicious confection, ideal for holiday mailing

4 cups rolled oats, uncooked
¾ cup evaporated milk
2½ cups marshmallows (40 cut in sixths or miniatures)
½ cup orange or pineapple juice
2 teaspoons cinnamon
1 teaspoon allspice

1 teaspoon nutmeg
2 teaspoons brandy flavoring
1 teaspoon salt
2 cups finely cut dates
1 pound mixed candied fruits
1 cup seedless raisins
1 cup grated coconut
1½ cups chopped nuts (omit if mailing far away)

Combine all ingredients well, using hands to mix. Shape into 1-inch balls or press in thin layer in buttered 9 × 13-inch pan. Let mellow at least 3 days before serving. Will keep indefinitely in refrigerator. If desired, dip balls in melted semi-sweet chocolate or fondant frosting. *4 dozen*

Decoration Ideas and Frostings

The ways in which cookies can be decorated are, quite literally, unlimited. Doughs, fillings, icings and toppings of sugar or coconut all may be tinted. Two thin wafers may be put together to make delicious cookie sandwiches. Special cutters or patterns give cookies fancy new shapes. Tidbits pressed into doughs before baking or set in frosting afterward give cookies gay faces.

Be they ball cookies or bar, drop cookies or rolled, there are ways to dress them up to make them fit any special occasion. And many of the decorations and frosting ideas are not complicated or time-consuming projects. In fact, they can be fun for the whole family—or a "cookie-baking committee"!

You'll find the following suggestions a source of ideas and you'll devise many other combinations on your own.

FOR BALL OR DROP COOKIES

Turn these into bonbon-like confections by making them small and dipping them, after baking, in thin Fondant Frosting or melted Chocolate Dip. If desired, sprinkle with coconut, colored sugar or crushed peppermint candies while frosting is "wet."

GLAZE FOR UNBAKED COOKIES

Brush on glaze before baking to hold nuts, candied fruits and colored sugars and candies in place.

COOKIE SANDWICHES

Thin crisp cookies put together with a frosting filling take on new elegance. Particularly good combinations are these:

Chocolate rolled cookies with Fudge Frosting, Coconut Frosting or Peppermint Frosting.

Sugar cookies with Fudge Frosting, Peanut Butter or Orange or Lemon Frosting.

Ginger or spice cookies with Lemon or Orange Frosting.
Fruit cookies with Cream Cheese Frosting, Orange or
Lemon Frosting, or Pineapple Frosting.
Nut cookies with Caramel Frosting, Sour Cream Frosting
or Toffee Frosting.

GLAZE FOR BAKED COOKIES

Dip baked, cooled cookies quickly into glaze kept melted over bowl
of hot water. If you wish to add decorations, press in place before
glaze hardens.

Rolled Cookies

These change character readily, depending on the size and
shape in which they are cut. For instance, they may be cut
king-size with the top of a coffee can and given gay faces
with raisins or chocolate chips to delight the children. Rolled
and cut in fancy shapes, decorated with thin frosting and colored candies, they go to the highest of teas! These suggestions
will give you ideas and methods for proceeding:

CUTTING

Aside from the many fancy cookie cutters available, you can make special patterns from cardboard. Cut out lightweight cardboard and place pattern on dough. Cut around pattern with point of knife. Pinked-edge cookies may be made by using pastry wheel or ravioli cutter.

Special Shapes for Special Occasions:

New Year's	New Year's bell
St. Valentine's	Hearts (large and small)
St. Patrick's Day	Shamrocks, 3-leaf clovers, Irish hats
Easter	Flowers, eggs, rabbits, chickens
Spring Teas	Flowers, butterflies
Bridal Shower	Wedding bells, bowknots, umbrellas, rings
Baby Shower	Rattles, balls, angels, umbrellas
Fourth of July	Firecrackers, drums
Halloween	Pumpkins, cats, broomsticks, witches
Christmas	Angels, stars, bells, wreaths, candles, Santas, Christmas trees, Christmas ornaments

DECORATING

To make fancy decorations or to write names, use pastry bag or special decorating kit, or use an ordinary envelope, sealed and cut off at one end. Place icing in the envelope, roll down top, make small hole in corner of envelope and force icing out by rolling top down tightly.

COLORING

Icings: Tinting, and flavoring as well, may be achieved by using such colorful liquids as blackberry, cherry, raspberry jam or preserves, or strong coffee, instead of food coloring. In tinting the icing, use just enough to give a good spreading consistency.

Doughs: Almost any light-colored cookie dough may be tinted successfully with food coloring and both novel and beautiful results are achieved in this way. Dough may be all tinted the same color or divided in halves or thirds, each portion being tinted a different pastel color to obtain striped, pinwheel, marbled or petal effects. Watch tinted doughs carefully so that overbrowning does not distort color.

Coconut: Add 1 or 2 drops of food coloring to 1 teaspoon of water and stir into coconut until well blended. Use only pastel colors!

Sugar: Color by adding 1 or 2 drops of cake coloring to ¼ cup sugar. Stir well, let dry and store in small covered bottle, ready to use. For decoration, sprinkle over cookie tops before baking or use on wet icing.

Sugar may be bought already colored, commercially prepared.

TOPPINGS

Unbaked cookies are colorfully and simply decorated with any of the following:

Colored candies, bought for decorating purposes.

Coconut. Press lightly into dough.

Crushed hard candy, such as peppermint sticks, lemon or orange drops.

Fruits, either candied, dried, or well-drained canned fruits. These are cut readily into flower, petal, pinwheel or other decorative shapes with kitchen shears or sharp pointed knife.

Shaved chocolate melts into an interesting glaze during baking.

Gumdrops, either sliced or whole small ones, pressed lightly into dough.

Nuts, chopped, halved or whole, toasted or not, as you prefer.

Seeds, such as poppy seed, sesame seed, caraway or anise, are good.

Sugar, colored or not, as you prefer. Sugar mixed with cinnamon or nutmeg is also good.

Baked cookies may be decorated with any of the above. Brush them with an egg white beaten just until foamy or spread them first with a soft frosting and decorate while frosting is still unset. Miniature marshmallows or snipped whole ones or shaved chocolate may also be used to decorate.

Rolled, ball or evenly shaped drop cookies are pretty with a glaze. If you want an opaque coating, use either the Fondant Frosting or the Decorator's Icing. If you want a clear glaze, brush cookies with a thin, syrup-type Glaze. Cookies may be glazed either before or after baking.

"Painted" Cookies

Names, faces or other ornamentation go readily onto baked cookies. Tint small amounts of undiluted evaporated milk with food coloring to obtain the desired color. Apply decoration with small, fine-tipped, clean camel's-hair paintbrush.

In addition to the drawing on of names or faces, this method may be used to make the fancy "marzipan"-type cookies—adding a pink blush to pear-shaped or apple-shaped cookies, brown lines and specks to a golden banana-cut cookie, etc., formed from light or tinted ball-type dough such as Baked Candy Cookies (see index).

Egg-yolk paint: Add 1 teaspoon water to 1 egg yolk and stir gently. Divide and tint as desired with food coloring. If mixtures thicken on standing, add a drop or two more of water. Very gay, intense colors may be achieved with this method. Apply to baked, cooled cookies with clean, fine-tipped brush.

FROSTINGS

In this chapter are recipes for these Good Frostings:

Baked-on	*Fondant*
Broiled	*Fudge*
Butter Cream	*Glaze (for baked cookies)*
Caramel	*Glaze (for unbaked cookies)*
Chocolate Dip	*Lemon*
Chocolate Frosting	*Meringue Topping*
Coconut	*(Baked-on)*
Coconut Meringue Topping	*Orange*
(Baked-on)	*Peanut Butter*
Coffee Frosting	*Peppermint*
Coffee Glaze	*Pineapple*
Cream Cheese	*Sour Cream*
Decorator's Icing	*Toffee*
Fluffy Fruit	

NOTE: Cookies that require individual frostings, toppings or fillings are shown in index under the names of the particular frosting, topping or filling.

Baked-on Frosting

Meringue-like

2 egg whites	½ teaspoon vanilla
¼ teaspoon salt	½ cup broken nut meats
1 cup sugar	

Beat egg whites and salt until foamy. Add sugar gradually, continuing to beat. Fold in vanilla and nuts. Spread on unbaked bar cookies or drop a small amount from a teaspoon on unbaked drop or rolled cookies. Bake at 350 or 375 degrees as directed for the cookies being frosted, allowing 20 to 25 minutes for baking. Cookies will bake more slowly because of moisture in frosting.

Particularly good on: almond bars, brownies, date bars, fruit bars, mincemeat bars, molasses bars, orange marmalade bars, pineapple bars, toffee bars, rolled butter cookies, chocolate cookies, fruit cookies, molasses cookies or sugar cookies.

Broiled Frosting

Quick party fare

2 tablespoons melted butter or margarine	½ cup brown sugar
	1 cup grated coconut
2 tablespoons evaporated milk	¼ teaspoon salt
	½ teaspoon vanilla

Combine well and spread on bar cookies after baking. Broil just until bubbly—watch closely, mixture burns easily. Let cool in pan as usual after cutting into squares.

Particularly good on: brownies, date bars, honey bars, mincemeat bars, molasses bars, orange marmalade bars, pineapple bars or raisin bars.

Butter Cream Frosting

Reliable goodness

4 tablespoons butter	1¼ cups sifted powdered sugar
2 tablespoons hot milk	
½ teaspoon vanilla	

Stir butter until very soft. Add a small amount of sugar, then milk and vanilla. Beat in remaining sugar until of soft, spreading consistency. Tint if desired. This frosting may be put through a decorator tube.

Particularly good on: Any baked cookie suitable for frosting.

Caramel Frosting

Similar to penuche

4 tablespoons butter or margarine	¼ teaspoon salt
	1 teaspoon vanilla
¼ cup evaporated milk	1½ cups sifted powdered
½ cup brown sugar	sugar

Combine butter, evaporated milk, brown sugar and salt. Cook over low heat until sugar is melted. Cool and stir in vanilla and powdered sugar. Spread on cooled, baked cookies. Sufficient for 9 × 13-inch pan of bar cookies, or 3 dozen drop or 4 dozen rolled cookies.

Particularly good on: butterscotch bars, date bars, mincemeat bars, molasses bars, pecan bars, raisin bars, toffee bars, butterscotch cookies, nut cookies, date drop cookies or peanut butter cookies.

Chocolate Dip

Fillip of flavor

1 cup semi-sweet chocolate bits	2 tablespoons milk, water or coffee
1 tablespoon butter or margarine	

Melt chocolate over very low heat, stirring to blend with butter and liquid. Set over warm water. Dip baked cookies (plain or frosted) into mixture. Set on rack or waxed paper until dip sets. Sufficient for 2 dozen.

Particularly good on: butter cookies, nut cookies, peppermint cookies, brown sugar cookies in ball, bar, dropped, icebox, pressed or roll types.

Chocolate Frosting

Gentlemen's choice

1 square unsweetened chocolate or 3 tablespoons cocoa

2 tablespoons melted butter or margarine

¼ cup evaporated milk or cream

¼ teaspoon salt

1 teaspoon vanilla

1½ to 2 cups sifted powdered sugar

Melt together chocolate and butter. Cool and add evaporated milk, salt and vanilla. Beat in sufficient powdered sugar to give proper spreading consistency. Spread on cooled, baked cookies. Spreads generously 9 × 13-inch pan of bar cookies (make half for 8 × 8-inch pan) or 5 dozen medium-size drop or rolled cookies.

Particularly good on: brownies, chocolate chip bars, orange marmalade, pecan or toffee bars or chocolate, oatmeal, peanut butter drop or rolled cookies, shortbread or sugar cookies.

Coconut Frosting

Magic with marshmallows

¼ cup boiling water

1 cup miniature marshmallows

2 tablespoons butter or margarine

1 cup grated coconut

Combine boiling water, marshmallows and butter and cook over low heat until marshmallows are melted. Stir in coconut and spread on cooled, baked cookies. Spreads 8- or 9-inch square pan of bar cookies or 2 dozen drop or rolled cookies. Icing stays soft.

Particularly good on: brownies, date bars, gumdrop squares, honey bars, orange marmalade bars, nut bars, or rolled chocolate, peanut butter or crisp sugar cookies.

Coconut Meringue Topping (Baked-on)

Golden crustiness

1 egg white	1 teaspoon vanilla
¼ teaspoon salt	½ cup grated coconut
1 cup sugar	

Beat egg white and salt until foamy. Gradually beat in sugar. Fold in vanilla and coconut. Spread on unbaked bar cookies. Bake at 350 degrees about 30 minutes. Sufficient for an 8- or 9-inch-square pan.

Particularly good on: brownies, butterscotch bars, date bars, fruit bars, honey bars or molasses bars.

Coffee Frosting

Wonderful for brunch cookies

¼ cup butter	1 tablespoon cream
1 egg yolk	2 to 2½ cups sifted
¼ teaspoon vanilla	powdered sugar
1½ teaspoons instant coffee	

Cream butter until very soft. Add ½ cup sugar, then stir in egg yolk, vanilla, coffee and cream. Beat smooth. Add sufficient of remaining sugar to make frosting thick enough to spread. Spreads 9 × 13-inch pan of baked bar cookies or about 5 dozen medium-size ball, drop or rolled cookies.

Particularly good on: chocolate, mocha, toffee cookies or any of the plain butter or sugar cookies.

Coffee Glaze

Quickly mixed

½ teaspoon instant coffee	1½ to 1¾ cups sifted
1½ tablespoons hot water	powdered sugar

Dissolve coffee powder in hot water. Stir in powdered sugar gradually for a thin glaze. Spread on cooled, baked cookies. Sufficient for 3 dozen medium-size ball, drop, icebox or rolled cookies.

Particularly good on: chocolate, mocha, toffee, vanilla-flavored butter or sugar cookies.

Cream Cheese Frosting

Deliciously rich

1 3-ounce package cream cheese	1½ cups sifted powdered sugar
2 tablespoons milk	¼ teaspoon salt
	½ teaspoon vanilla

Beat cream cheese until fluffy. Stir in remaining ingredients, blending well. Spread on cooled, baked cookies. Spreads 9 × 13-inch pan of bar cookies or 3 dozen medium-size drop cookies.

Particularly good on: brownies, date bars, honey bars, fruit bars, mincemeat bars, molasses bars, orange marmalade bars, pecan bars, raisin bars or chocolate, date, honey or fruit rolled or drop cookies.

Decorator's Icing

For one touch of glamor

2 egg whites	2½ to 3 cups sifted
⅛ teaspoon cream of tartar	powdered sugar
2 teaspoons water	

Blend egg whites, cream of tartar and water and beat until frothy; gradually add powdered sugar. Beat until mixture holds soft peaks. Tint as desired with food coloring. May be put through decorator tube or spread with spatula.

Particularly good on: Frosted cookies when a rosette or name is added for decoration. May be used as adhesive in building a Gingerbread House.

Fluffy Fruit Frosting

Picnic specialty

½ cup apricot purée or crushed pineapple	1½ cups sifted powdered sugar
1 3-ounce package cream cheese	

Whip fruit and cream cheese together until fluffy. Stir in powdered sugar, adding more if necessary for proper consistency. Spread on cooled, baked cookies. Sufficient for 9 × 13-inch pan of bar cookies or 3 dozen ball, drop or rolled cookies.

Particularly good on: date bars, fruit bars, honey bars, gumdrop squares, oatmeal cookies, mincemeat cookies, molasses cookies, orange cookies, nut cookies or raisin cookies.

Fondant Frosting

Quick-change favorite

2 tablespoons melted butter or margarine

2 tablespoons milk, water, fruit juice or coffee

1½ cups sifted powdered sugar

¼ teaspoon salt

½ teaspoon vanilla

Food coloring, if desired

Combine ingredients and blend well. Dip cooled, baked cookies into frosting. Set on rack or waxed paper until frosting sets. While still soft, frosting may be sprinkled with coconut, colored sugar, crushed peppermint candies or finely chopped nuts. Sufficient for 3 dozen cookies.

Particularly good on: brownies, butter cookies, fruit bars, lemon cookies, orange cookies, raisin cookies, sour cream cookies, sugar cookies, nut cookies, honey cookies and molasses cookies.

Fudge Frosting

Quick and delicious

1 6-ounce package semisweet chocolate bits

¼ cup evaporated milk or cream

Melt chocolate in cream over very low heat, stirring to blend. Cool to spreading consistency. Spread on cooled, baked 8- or 9-inch-square pan of bar cookies or 2 dozen ball, drop or rolled cookies.

Particularly good on: brownies, chocolate chip bars, oatmeal, nut or crisp sugar cookies.

Glaze (for baked cookies)

For satiny sheen

½ cup corn syrup   ½ cup water
½ cup sugar

Combine ingredients and stir over low heat until sugar is dissolved. Boil without stirring until mixture is thick and will spin a thread. Dip cooled, baked cookies quickly in glaze kept melted over a bowl of hot water. Sufficient to coat about 3 dozen cookies.

Particularly good on: firm ball, drop, icebox or rolled cookies of dominant flavors such as seed cookies, spice cookies, honey cookies, molasses cookies or fruit cookies.

Glaze (for unbaked cookies)

A professional touch

2 egg whites
⅛ teaspoon salt
Sugar, if desired

Beat egg whites just until foamy. Add salt. Brush over unbaked cookies. Sprinkle with a small amount of white or colored sugar before baking, if desired.

Particularly good on: Firm ball, icebox or rolled cookies. May be used on press cookies to aid in securing decorations of candied fruits, colored sugars or shaved nuts.

Lemon Frosting

Piquant flavor

2 tablespoons soft butter or margarine	Juice and grated rind of 1 lemon
1½ cups sifted powdered sugar	¼ teaspoon salt

Blend butter and sugar. Beat in lemon juice, rind and salt. Spread on cooled, baked cookies. Sufficient for 9 × 13-inch pan of bar cookies or 3 to 4 dozen drop or rolled cookies.

Particularly good on: date bars, fruit bars, oatmeal bars, mincemeat bars, honey cookies, molasses cookies, orange cookies, pineapple cookies, raisin cookies or sugar cookies.

Meringue Topping (Baked-on)

Nut-rich

1 egg white	½ teaspoon vanilla
¼ teaspoon salt	¼ cup chopped nuts
½ cup brown sugar	

Beat egg white and salt until foamy. Gradually beat in brown sugar. Fold in vanilla and nuts. Spread on unbaked bar cookies. Bake at 350 or 375 degrees as directed for the particular cookie on which used for 20 to 25 minutes. Meringue may be dropped on rolled or icebox cookies before baking. Bake at suggested temperature until meringue is firm and browned, usually slightly longer than for undecorated cookies. Spreads 8- or 9-inch-square pan of bar cookies or 2 dozen large rolled cookies.

Particularly good on: brownies, date bars, fruit bars, honey bars, mincemeat bars, molasses bars, orange marmalade bars, pineapple bars, raisin bars, icebox or rolled honey cookies, chocolate cookies, fruit cookies or sugar cookies.

Orange Frosting

Eye- and taste-pleasing

4 tablespoons butter or
margarine
1 egg, beaten
Juice and grated rind of 1
small orange

¼ teaspoon salt
2 cups sifted powdered
sugar

Combine all ingredients, beating until fluffy. Add more powdered sugar if needed for spreading consistency. Covers generously 9 × 13-inch pan of bar cookies or 4 dozen ball, icebox, drop or rolled cookies.

Particularly good on: date cookies, fruit cookies, nut cookies, oatmeal cookies, mincemeat cookies, molasses cookies, pineapple cookies, sour cream cookies or sugar cookies.

Peanut Butter Frosting

Delightful variety

¼ cup peanut butter
2 tablespoons melted but-
ter or margarine
½ cup brown sugar

2 tablespoons hot coffee
1½ cups sifted powdered
sugar
½ teaspoon vanilla

Combine peanut butter, butter, brown sugar and hot coffee. Stir over low heat until sugar is dissolved. Cool slightly, then stir in powdered sugar and vanilla. Spread on baked and cooled cookies. Sufficient for 8- or 9-inch-square pan of bar cookies or 3 dozen medium-size individual cookies.

Particularly good on: brownies, oatmeal cookies, gumdrop cookies, date bars or sugar cookies.

Peppermint Frosting

Mint-candy crunchy

3 tablespoons butter or margarine

2 tablespoons cream or evaporated milk

1½ cups sifted powdered sugar

Red food coloring, if desired

½ cup crushed peppermint candy

Combine butter and cream and beat in powdered sugar gradually. Tint, if desired. Add crushed candy and spread on cooled, baked cookies. Spreads 8- or 9-inch pan of bar cookies or 3 dozen medium-size individual cookies.

Particularly good on: brownies, chocolate cookies, butter cookies, sour cream cookies, nut cookies or sugar cookies.

Pineapple Frosting

Hawaiian specialty

¼ cup butter or margarine

¼ cup crushed pineapple and juice

1½ cups sifted powdered sugar

1 teaspoon grated orange or lemon rind

Cream butter. Blend in pineapple, powdered sugar and grated rind. Beat until fluffy. Spread on cooled, baked cookies. Sufficient for 8- or 9-inch pan of bar cookies or 3 dozen individual cookies.

Particularly good on: date bars, fruit bars, honey bars, gumdrop cookies, oatmeal cookies, orange cookies, nut cookies, sour cream cookies or sugar cookies. Especially useful for making cookie sandwiches of two thin, crisp cookies such as Rolled Sugar Cookies or Icebox Nut Cookies with Pineapple Frosting as filling.

Sour Cream Frosting

Tangy-sweet and smooth

1 cup commercial sour cream	1 teaspoon grated orange or lemon rind
2 cups sifted powdered sugar	

Combine ingredients and beat until fluffy. Spread on cooled, baked cookies. Sufficient to spread generously 9 × 13-inch pan of bar cookies or 4 dozen medium-size individual cookies.

Particularly good on: brownies, date cookies, fruit cookies, mincemeat cookies, molasses cookies, chocolate cookies. Effective when a glaze-type icing is desired.

Toffee Frosting

Blended flavors

4 tablespoons butter or margarine	2 cups sifted powdered sugar
½ cup brown sugar	1 teaspoon brandy or vanilla flavoring
¼ cup hot coffee	
2 tablespoons cream or evaporated milk	

Combine butter, brown sugar, coffee and evaporated milk. Cook over low heat until sugar is melted. Cool, then stir in powdered sugar and flavoring. Spread on cooled, baked cookies. Sufficient to spread 9 × 13-inch pan of bar cookies (half of recipe is enough for an 8- or 9-inch-square pan) or 4 to 5 dozen individual cookies.

Particularly good on: butterscotch cookies, date cookies, nut cookies, molasses cookies, sugar cookies or vanilla-flavored butter cookies.

Let's Plan a Party

A good party becomes better when refreshments include tasty cookies. Star of many a tea-and-coffee party, cookies also belong rightfully to such gala events as wedding receptions, a grand ball or that friendly American occasion, the "at-home."

Although there may be a uniformed helper in the kitchen on party day, most hostesses prefer to serve homemade goodies. And rightly so. Plan for cookies, then, that may be made ahead. Many freeze perfectly—in either a baked or raw state. Some improve with aging. Some may be made ahead and decorated later.

Select cookies for a range of flavors. All frosted cookies would be as dull as a variety with no frosting at all.

Decorations include colored sugars, candies, candied fruits, preserves, as well as nut meats—and it is magical how a bit of colored sugar on a plain rolled cookie cut in a small size can put an old favorite into fancy dress.

Consider, too, different shapes for the familiar recipes. Form triangles or diamonds instead of all round wafers. Include some curved crescents as well as ball cookies. And certainly make use of the prettiest forms that the cookie press will make. Not to be overlooked are the attractive, tiny wreath cookies made with a star plate from plain, tinted or chocolate doughs.

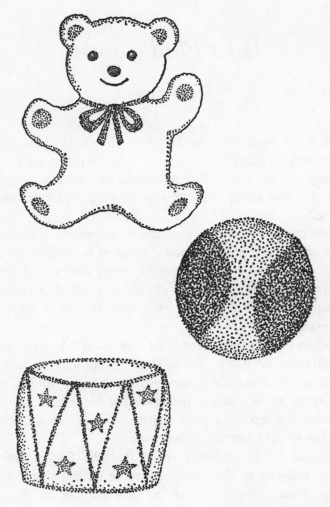

Teddy bear—Tinted frosting decoration. *Drum*—Tinted frosting decoration. *Ball*—Frosting decoration.

PARTY COOKIE ASSORTMENT

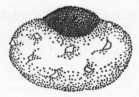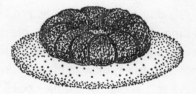

Chocolate Filled Balls (page 111) Picture Cookies (page 155)

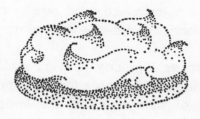

Macaroon-Topped Butter Cookies (page 153)

Cookie Napoleons decorated with chocolate glaze, candied cherry and almond slivers (page 148)

Party cookies may be created from plain doughs by such simple additions, before baking, as finely cut bits of glazed fruits. The famous Danish Wreath cookies are fashioned thus.

Glazing cookies gives them a bright party look, too. Before baking, formed cookies are glazed by brushing with slightly beaten egg white or a combination of egg white and a tablespoon of water, or with plain milk.

After baking, brushing cookies, while still slightly warm, with a very thin powdered sugar and fruit juice icing or powdered sugar mixed with milk gives a transparent glaze—somewhat heavier, of course, than the baked-on kind.

And if you've never served filled cookies or small, thin wafers put together sandwich-style at a party, you've a new treat in store.

Generally, cookies for party fare are made small—even one-bite size—particularly if made for a stand-up affair with much circulating of guests during the refreshment hour. However, there are occasions when giant cookies would be more in keeping: refreshments served a roundup of youngsters after a swimming party, for instance, when there are young appetites to satisfy.

Ease of eating might be a factor in selection for a specific party, because cookies are finger food. Consider the lady's gown—avoid offering cookies too soft for easy holding or those that might dust snowy powdered sugar over her best basic black. Gentlemen abhor tidbits that seem to melt in the hand and with which the tiny napkins supplied at party gatherings are inadequate to cope.

Cookies can be made to emphasize a color scheme, to fit a theme, to be a decorative centerpiece as well as a tasty mouthful. Serve Frosted Snowballs after a wintry sledding jaunt, Orange Marmalade Bars at a bridal shower and Almond Kisses at a farewell party, for instance.

Point up themes with special shapes in Picture Cookies for a dinner-party centerpiece, with pressed or cutout animal cookies and Circus Mint Cookies for a children's table, with cutout cookies for special occasions. Use hearts and cupids for Valentine's Day; bunnies and eggs for Easter (shape the eggs from ball dough, if desired); pumpkins and cats, witches and leaves for Halloween; and so on through the calendar's special holidays. Additional suggestions will be found in the chapter entitled "Decoration Ideas and Frostings."

Party cookie baking means something a little out of the ordinary. It may be simply a perfectly blended dough such as Rich Rolled Cookies made with seven (yes, seven!) egg yolks or a fancy three-layer confection like Cookie Napoleons.

Plan a variety from the following suggestions and be sure of cookie platters that rate you a social and culinary success.

In this chapter are recipes for these Good Cookies:

PLAIN   FANCY

BALL

Brown Velvet Balls   Baked Candy Cookies
Cherry Tops   Cherry Crowns
Currant Crisps   Chocolate-filled Balls
Frosted Snowballs   Crested Coconut Oatmeal
Mocha Balls   Balls
Nut Cakes   Filled Chocolate Flake
Print Shortbread   Balls
                              Golden Coconut Balls
                              Meringue-frosted Balls
                              Pastel Nuggets
                              Rum Party Wafers

PLAIN   FANCY

BARS

Almond Bars   Orange Marmalade
Brownies III   Bars II
Chinese Chews
Pecan Bars
Spice Honey Bars

LAYERED BARS

Almond Meringue Bars
Coconut Dream Bars
Date Layered Bars
Jam Crackies
Matrimonial Bars
Meringue Jam Bars
Meringue Nut Bars
Mocha Nut Bars

DROP

Lemon Chips   Almond Kisses
Macaroons   Brown Sugar Kisses
   (Coconut)   Cherry Coconut Balls
Pecan Crisps   Lace Cookies
Pecan Macaroons   Maple Sugar Crisps
                                         Oatmeal Coconut Cherry
                                            Crisps
                                         Orange Buttermilk
                                            Frosted Cookies
                                         Pineapple Macaroons
                                         Rice Flour Almondettes
                                         Sesame Brown Sugar Drops

FILLED

Date-filled Rolled Cookies
Mocha-filled Cookies
Phoebe's Fig-filled Cookies
Thimble Tarts

PLAIN   FANCY

ICEBOX

Almond Wafers
Spiced Almond Wafers
Anise Crisps
Black Walnut Fingers
Lemon Bars
Orange Nut Slices

Chocolate Mint Icebox
    Cookies
Cinnamon Chocolate Thins

NO-BAKE

No-bake Dream Bars
Quick Unbaked Brownies

PRESSED

Cream Cheese Almond
    Bars
Wreath Cookies
Lemon Wafers

ROLLED

Brazilian Treats
Punch Bowl Cookies
Rich Nut Sticks
Rich Rolled Cookies

Almond Cream Sandwiches
Almond Paste-topped
    Butter Cookies
Chocolate Scallops
Circus Mint Cookies
Cookie Napoleons
Filled Butter Rings
Filled Silhouette Cookies
Ice Cream Cookie Cups
Jelly-filled Rings
Macaroon-topped Butter
    Cookies
Minted Chocolate Wafers
Orange Cream Sandwiches
Picture Cookies

Other recipes that could be included in this category are the following (to locate, see index):

BARS
> *Cherry Cheese Dreams*

DROP
> *Brown Sugar Nut Crisps*
> *Pineapple Cone Cookies*

FILLED
> *Georgia's Briars*

ICEBOX
> *Pinwheel Cookies*

NO-BAKE
> *Bourbon Balls*

PRESSED
> *Crown Cookies*

ROLLED
> *Butter Rings*
> *Chocolate Dollars*
> *Crescents*

BALL COOKIES

Baked Candy Cookies [FANCY]

Cookie covering for candied fruits or chocolate mints

⅓ cup butter (do not substitute)	2 teaspoons vanilla
⅔ cup sifted powdered sugar	1¼ cups sifted cake flour
	Food coloring, if desired

Blend soft butter with powdered sugar and vanilla. Add a drop or two of food coloring, if desired. Gradually stir in flour in about four portions. Wrap 1 tablespoon of dough around a candied cherry, bit of candied pineapple, pitted date or chocolate mint.

If a two-color cookie is desired, divide dough and add food coloring to one portion. Use a small ball of tinted dough for center and wrap with layer of plain-colored dough. Bake on ungreased sheet at 350 degrees about 12 to 15 minutes. Cool.

Dough may be shaped in crescents, squares, triangles or diamonds instead of balls, if preferred. Frost cooled cookies with white, tinted or chocolate Decorating Icing. Garnish with shaved nuts, flaked coconut, colored sugar, grated chocolate or colored icing put through decorating tube. *About 1½ dozen*

Chocolate Dough Variation: Add 1 ounce or square melted, cooled chocolate to butter mixture. Use ½ ounce chocolate if basic dough is divided and only one portion is to be chocolate-flavored.

Butterscotch Dough Variation: Use ½ cup brown sugar, firmly packed, instead of powdered sugar.

Candy Cookie Decorating Icing

A smooth frosting in which to dip cookies

1 cup sifted powdered sugar
1½ tablespoons hot milk
1 teaspoon vanilla or ½ teaspoon almond or lemon extract

1 ounce or square unsweetened chocolate, if chocolate icing is desired (flavor with vanilla)

Blend all ingredients. If too thin, add additional powdered sugar. If too thick, thin to desired consistency with a few additional drops of milk or water.

To frost, dip cookies into frosting (holding with fingers), decorate, if desired, and place on rack or waxed paper to dry.

These candy cookies are attractive when served in small pleated paper cups like miniature petits fours.

Brown Velvet Balls [PLAIN]

The intriguing flavor comes from browned butter and cardamom

1 cup butter, browned	½ teaspoon baking powder
2 cups sugar	½ teaspoon ground
1 egg	cardamom
2½ cups sifted all-purpose	⅔ cup chopped nuts
flour	

Melt butter and cook until lightly browned. Allow to cool. Stir in sugar and slightly beaten egg. Sift baking powder with flour and stir in cardamom. Add to butter mixture. Stir in nuts. Form ¾-inch balls. Place on ungreased baking sheet. Bake at 350 degrees about 12 to 15 minutes. *5 dozen*

Cherry Crowns [FANCY]

Very rich, butter-flavored balls, topped with cherries

1 cup butter	2½ cups sifted all-purpose
1 3-ounce package cream	flour
cheese	1 egg white
1 cup sugar	1 cup finely ground,
1 egg yolk	unblanched almonds
1 teaspoon almond extract	Candied cherries for garnish

Blend together soft butter and room-temperature cheese until smooth. Add sugar, then slightly beaten egg yolk and almond extract. Stir in flour. Chill dough, if necessary, to make easily handled mixture. Form into 1-inch balls, dipping tops in slightly beaten egg white. Dip in ground almonds. Place on cookie sheet and bake at 350 degrees about 15 minutes.

Remove from oven and press half a candied cherry, round side up, into center of cookie. Press gently to avoid shattering cookies. *About 4½ dozen*

Cherry Tops [PLAIN]

Rich, pretty, but easy to make

½ cup butter	½ teaspoon vanilla
½ cup sugar	¼ teaspoon salt
1 egg	1½ cups sifted cake flour
¼ teaspoon almond extract	Candied cherries for garnish

Cream butter and sugar. Blend in beaten egg and flavorings. Sift dry ingredients and add. Chill dough 30 minutes. Form into 1-inch balls. Top each with a bit of candied cherry. Bake on ungreased sheet at 375 degrees 10 to 12 minutes. *About 3½ dozen*

Frosted Variation: Bake plain balls without topping. Frost with melted dipping chocolate or sweet chocolate. Garnish with chopped nuts or flaked coconut.

Nut Variation: Top dough with whole pecan, filbert or blanched almond in place of cherry. Omit almond extract and use 1 teaspoon vanilla.

Chocolate-filled Balls [FANCY]

Very impressive-looking—and tasting!

½ cup butter	1 cup sifted all-purpose
¼ cup brown sugar	flour
1 egg yolk	1 egg white
1 teaspoon vanilla	1 cup finely ground nuts
	Chocolate Filling

Cream butter. Blend in brown sugar. Add egg yolk and vanilla. Stir in flour. Chill dough 30 minutes. Form 1-inch balls. Dip in slightly beaten egg white, then in ground nuts. Place on lightly greased cookie sheet. Make a slight depression in center with tip of teaspoon or finger. Bake at 300 degrees 20 to 25 minutes. Cool and fill depression with Chocolate Filling. *2 dozen small cookies*

Chocolate Filling:

1 tablespoon butter
¾ cup semi-sweet chocolate pieces

1 teaspoon vanilla or ½ teaspoon rum extract
2 tablespoons corn syrup
1 tablespoon water

Melt butter and chocolate over hot water. Stir in corn syrup and water until smooth and thickened. Cool, add flavoring.

Crested Coconut Oatmeal Balls [FANCY]

Coconut-coated 'n' decorated with preserves

¾ cup shortening
¾ cup brown sugar, firmly packed
1 egg
1 teaspoon vanilla
1½ cups sifted all-purpose flour

½ teaspoon salt
½ teaspoon baking powder
1½ cups rolled oats
1 cup flaked or cut shredded coconut
Jam, preserves or jelly for filling

Blend brown sugar into soft shortening until fluffy. Beat in egg and vanilla. Sift together flour, salt and baking powder and stir in gradually. Add rolled oats, mixing well. Chill dough 1 hour. Form 1-inch balls. Roll in finely cut coconut. Place balls on ungreased cookie sheet. With tip of teaspoon or finger, make slight depression in center of each ball. Fill with a bit of colorful jam or preserves (berry, peach, apricot, plum or currant, mint or grape jelly). Bake at 350 degrees about 10 minutes. *About 3 dozen*

⌐Currant Crisps [PLAIN]

The crispness of a butter cookie with the chewiness of currants

½ cup butter or margarine
¾ cup sifted powdered
  sugar
1 egg, slightly beaten
1½ cups sifted all-purpose
  flour

¼ teaspoon salt
1 teaspoon baking powder
½ cup currants
½ teaspoon vanilla

Cream butter well. Blend in sugar. Stir in egg, mixing thoroughly. Sift together dry ingredients and add, working with hands if necessary to form dough. Add currants and vanilla. Pinch off balls of dough and pat ¼ inch thick on ungreased cookie sheet. Prick with fork. Bake at 350 degrees just until golden, about 10 to 12 minutes. *3 dozen*

Filled Chocolate Flake Balls [FANCY]

Surprisingly good combination of fruit and chocolate

½ cup butter
½ cup sugar
1 teaspoon vanilla
1½ cups sifted all-purpose
  flour
¼ teaspoon baking powder
½ teaspoon salt

2 tablespoons sweet or sour
  cream
¼ cup grated semi-sweet
  chocolate
Apricot, peach or orange
  marmalade
Butter Cream Frosting

Cream butter. Add sugar, blending well. Add vanilla. Sift together dry ingredients and add alternately with cream. Stir in grated chocolate. Form 1-inch balls. Depress center of balls with teaspoon or fingertip. Bake at 375 degrees 10 minutes on ungreased cookie sheet. Cool. Fill hollow center with marmalade. Frost, if desired, with orange-tinted Butter Cream

Frosting (use 2 drops yellow food coloring and 1 of red for orange tint). *3 dozen*

Frosted Snowballs [PLAIN]

Crisp oatmeal balls to frost festively

¾ cup margarine
½ cup brown sugar, firmly packed
1 teaspoon lemon extract
1½ cups sifted all-purpose flour

¼ teaspoon salt
1 cup rolled oats
Decorator's Icing
Flake coconut

Cream margarine until soft, then add sugar, beating until smooth. Stir in lemon extract, then sifted flour and salt. Add rolled oats. Form dough in walnut-sized balls. Bake on ungreased sheet at 325 degrees until dough is baked through, about 15 to 20 minutes. Cool. Frost with Decorator's Icing and roll in flaked or snipped shredded coconut. *About 3½ dozen*

Golden Coconut Balls [FANCY]

Fruitcake-like confection

1 egg
½ cup brown sugar
1 cup finely chopped nuts
½ cup chopped dates

1½ cups flaked or cut, shredded coconut
Candied red and green cherries

Beat egg, then blend in sugar. Stir in nuts, dates and half of coconut. Form 1 tablespoon of dough around half a candied cherry. Roll balls in remaining coconut. Bake on greased cookie sheet at 350 degrees about 8 minutes or just until coconut is tinged golden brown. Carefully remove from sheet while hot. Cool on rack. *About 2 dozen*

Meringue-frosted Balls [FANCY]

Snow-capped butter-nut balls

1 cup butter
¾ cup sugar
2 egg yolks
1 teaspoon vanilla
1⅔ cups sifted all-purpose flour

1 cup ground nuts (almonds, filberts, pecans or walnuts)
2 egg whites
2 tablespoons sugar, additional
Glazed cherries for garnish

Blend soft butter and ¾ cup sugar together. Beat in egg yolks and vanilla well. Mix nut meats with flour. Add to butter mixture in three parts, working in thoroughly. Chill 1 hour. Form in small balls about the size of a walnut. Beat egg whites stiff. Beat in 2 tablespoons sugar. Top each ball cookie with a bit of meringue. Garnish with a bit of glazed cherry. Bake on ungreased sheet at 350 degrees 12 to 15 minutes. *About 3½ dozen*

Mocha Balls [PLAIN]

Coffee-flavored dough with bits of chocolate baked in

1 cup shortening
1 cup white sugar
½ cup brown sugar, firmly packed
1¼ teaspoons vanilla
2 eggs
1 teaspoon baking powder

1 teaspoon salt
2 teaspoons powdered instant coffee
2¼ cups sifted all-purpose flour
1 pound dipping chocolate

Cream shortening until soft. Blend in sugars well. Beat in vanilla and eggs. Sift together dry ingredients and add to mixture. Cut dipping chocolate into coarse chunks. Add to batter, stirring just to blend. Chill dough 30 minutes. Form in 1-inch balls. Place on lightly greased baking sheet. Bake at 350 degrees 10 minutes. *About 4½ dozen*

Nut Cakes [PLAIN]

Crisp, macaroon-like nut cookies

¼ teaspoon salt
6 egg whites
2¾ cups sifted brown sugar

1 teaspoon vanilla
1 pound ground nut meats
    (about 4 cups chopped)

Beat egg whites and salt together until stiff. Gradually beat in brown sugar, then vanilla. Fold in finely ground nut meats. Drop by teaspoonfuls in granulated sugar. Place balls on greased baking sheet. Bake at 325 degrees until firm, about 25 minutes. *5 dozen*

Pastel Nuggets [FANCY]

Delicately flavored with brown sugar and orange rind

1 cup butter or margarine
½ cup brown sugar, firmly
    packed
1 egg
1 teaspoon vanilla
2 teaspoons grated orange
    rind

3 cups sifted all-purpose
    flour
½ teaspoon salt
1 cup rolled oats
White and tinted Decorat-
    or's Icing or Butter Cream
    Frosting

Cream butter, blend in sugar, egg, vanilla and grated orange rind. Stir in sifted flour and salt gradually. Work in oats thoroughly. Shape in 48 small balls. Bake on ungreased sheet at 350 degrees 12 to 15 minutes. Cool. Frost with variously pastel-colored Butter Cream Frosting or Decorator's Icing. *4 dozen*

Print Shortbread [PLAIN]

To make with an old-fashioned wooden cookie "print" or springerle board

1 cup butter	2 cups sifted all-purpose
½ cup sifted powdered	flour
sugar	¼ teaspoon baking powder
1 teaspoon vanilla	

Cream butter thoroughly. Gradually beat in sugar, then vanilla. Sift together baking powder and flour and stir in. Chill dough 30 minutes. Form 1-inch balls. Place on ungreased cookie sheet. Press balls of dough with small well-floured cookie print to slightly less than ¼ inch thick or press square of dough with well-floured springerle board to ¼ inch thick, trimming away edges. Prick dough with fork, if baking in square, so that it will not buckle during baking, and cut into squares. Bake at 375 degrees about 8 minutes. (If using springerle board, re-cut cookies when removed from oven.) *About 4 dozen*

Rum Party Wafers [FANCY]

Rum chocolates inside, shaved nuts outside

¾ cup butter	3½ cups sifted all-purpose
1½ cups sugar	flour
2 eggs	¼ cup sweet or sour heavy
1 teaspoon vanilla	cream
1½ teaspoons baking	2 7-ounce packages thin
powder	chocolate rum wafers, the
½ teaspoon salt	hard, flat kind

Cream soft butter and sugar together. Add slightly beaten eggs and vanilla. Sift together dry ingredients and add alternately with sour cream. Chill dough 30 minutes. Wrap

1 tablespoon dough around each thin chocolate rum wafer, completely covering candy. Place on ungreased baking sheet. Sprinkle a few slivered almonds or finely chopped pecans or filberts or shaved Brazil nuts on top for garnish, if desired. Bake at 375 degrees 10 minutes. Avoid overbrowning. *About 5 dozen*

BAR COOKIES

Almond Bars [PLAIN]

Delicately flavored with grated almonds and orange rind

¼ cup melted butter or margarine	1 teaspoon baking powder
	¼ teaspoon salt
1 cup sugar	1 cup grated blanched
1 egg, beaten	almonds
1 cup sifted all-purpose flour	1 teaspoon grated orange rind

Blend butter and sugar thoroughly. Add egg. Sift together dry ingredients and stir in. Add almonds and orange rind. Spread in buttered 8-inch-square pan. Bake at 350 degrees 20 minutes. Good frosted with orange or other fruit-flavored icing (see index). *2 dozen*

Brownies III [PLAIN]

Lighter, tender cake-type

½ cup shortening
1 cup sugar
2 eggs
2 squares or ounces melted
chocolate

1 cup sifted all-purpose
flour
¼ teaspoon salt
¼ teaspoon baking soda
½ cup chopped nuts
1 teaspoon vanilla

Cream shortening and sugar well. Add beaten eggs, then melted, cooled chocolate. Sift together dry ingredients and fold in. Fold in nuts. Then add vanilla. Pour into greased 8-inch-square pan. Bake at 325 degrees about 30 minutes or until top springs back when pressed lightly with finger. Cool on rack 10 to 15 minutes, then cut into squares. Dust with powdered sugar or frost, if desired. *2 dozen*

Chinese Chews [PLAIN]

If you like chewy cookies, you'll love these fruit bars

1 cup sifted all-purpose
flour
1 cup sugar
½ teaspoon salt
1 teaspoon baking powder
1 cup chopped nuts
1 cup chopped dates

½ cup chopped maraschino
cherries
2 eggs, beaten
¼ cup melted butter
1 teaspoon grated lemon
rind

Sift together flour, sugar, salt and baking powder. Add nuts, dates and cherries. Combine with eggs, melted butter and lemon rind. Pour into greased 8-inch-square pan. Bake at 325 degrees about 25 minutes. *2 dozen*

Orange Marmalade Bars II [FANCY]

Unusual—with orange marmalade for flavor, graham cracker crumbs for "crunch"

⅔ cup butter or margarine
1 cup sugar
2 eggs
1¾ cups sifted all-purpose flour
1 teaspoon salt

½ teaspoon baking powder
1 cup graham cracker crumbs
¼ cup melted butter
1 cup chopped nuts
1 cup orange marmalade

Cream butter and sugar well. Add eggs one at a time. Sift together flour, salt and baking powder and stir in. Press into 9 × 12-inch pan. Combine graham cracker crumbs, melted butter and nuts. Sprinkle over dough. Drop orange marmalade by spoonfuls over crumbs. Bake at 375 degrees 25 to 30 minutes. Cut into bars when cool. *3 dozen*

Pecan Bars [PLAIN]

Rich-flavored with brown sugar, butter and pecans

¼ cup butter
1 cup brown sugar
2 eggs
⅔ cup sifted cake flour
½ teaspoon baking powder

¼ teaspoon salt
1 teaspoon vanilla
1 cup coarsely chopped pecans

Cream butter. Blend in brown sugar. Add eggs one at a time, beating well. Sift together dry ingredients and fold in gently. Add vanilla and nuts. Bake in lightly greased 8-inch-square pan at 350 degrees about 30 minutes. Cut into bars while warm. *3 dozen*

Spice Honey Bars [PLAIN]

Crunchy and chewy with chopped fruit, nuts and cracker crumbs

1 cup chopped dates or figs	½ cup sifted all-purpose
1 cup chopped nuts	flour
2 eggs, beaten	½ cup finely crushed gra-
¾ cup honey	ham cracker crumbs
	¼ teaspoon salt

Combine dates and nuts. Beat eggs until light, gradually beating in honey. Fold in sifted flour. Add crumbs, then dates, nuts and salt. Bake in greased 8-inch-square pan at 350 degrees about 35 minutes. Cut into squares when cool.
2 dozen

LAYERED BARS

Almond Meringue Bars [FANCY]

Like shortbread on the bottom, macaroons on the top

Bottom Layer:

1 cup white sugar	1½ cups sifted all-purpose
3 tablespoons butter or	flour
margarine	1 teaspoon baking powder
	2 egg yolks

Combine sugar and butter, beating well. Sift together dry ingredients and add. Blend in egg yolks. Spread evenly in lightly buttered 8-inch-square pan.

Top Layer:

2 egg whites
¾ cup powdered sugar

1 cup blanched chopped
  almonds
¼ teaspoon salt

Beat egg whites until stiff. Gradually beat in powdered sugar. Fold in nuts and salt. Spread over bottom layer. Bake at 350 degrees about 25 minutes. Cool and cut into squares. *2 dozen*

Coconut Dream Bars [FANCY]

Perennial favorite two-layer bar

Bottom Layer:

1 cup sifted all-purpose
  flour

½ cup butter
½ cup brown sugar

Cream together butter and sugar and add flour. Press in thin layer in 9-inch-square pan. Bake at 325 degrees 10 minutes. Add topping.

Topping:

1 cup brown sugar
2 eggs, beaten
1 teaspoon vanilla
¼ teaspoon salt

2 tablespoons flour
1 teaspoon baking powder
1 cup chopped nuts
1½ cups grated coconut

Blend sugar and beaten eggs. Add vanilla. Sift together salt, flour and baking powder and stir in. Add nuts and coconut. Spread over first baked layer, return to 325-degree oven and bake 10 minutes more. Cut into squares while warm. *3 dozen*

Date Layered Bars [FANCY]

Orange marmalade and chopped dates makes a fabulous topping for these

Bottom Layer:

1 cup sifted all-purpose flour	½ cup butter or margarine
	½ teaspoon vanilla

Work together till blended into smooth dough. Press into 9 × 12-inch pan. Bake at 350 degrees 12 minutes. Spread with topping.

Topping:

2 eggs, beaten	2 tablespoons flour
⅓ cup orange marmalade	½ teaspoon baking powder
1 cup brown sugar	¼ teaspoon salt
1 cup chopped pitted dates	½ teaspoon vanilla
1 cup chopped nuts	

Combine all ingredients in order given. Spread over baked mixture and continue baking at 350 degrees till topping is firm and browned, about 25 minutes. Cut into squares while warm. *3 dozen*

Jam Crackies [FANCY]

Fruit and cheese—always good—especially as a 3-layer cookie

½ cup butter or margarine
½ cup grated cheddar cheese (do not use process cheese)
1 cup sugar
2 eggs
1 teaspoon cinnamon

3 cups sifted all-purpose flour
½ teaspoon salt
1 teaspoon baking powder
1½ cups strawberry, raspberry, youngberry or blackberry preserves

Blend butter, cheese, sugar and eggs, then sift together dry ingredients and add. Spread half the dough in 8-inch-square pan. Cover with preserves. Sprinkle with remaining dough. Bake at 375 degrees 30 to 35 minutes. Cool before cutting into squares. *2 dozen*

Matrimonial Bars [FANCY]

Delicious date-centered 3-layer bar

Bottom Layer:

1¼ cups sifted all-purpose flour
½ teaspoon salt
1 teaspoon baking powder

½ teaspoon baking soda
1¼ cups rolled oats
¾ cup butter or margarine

Sift together dry ingredients. Add oats. Cut in butter or margarine till pieces resemble coarse corn meal. Press half the dough into 9 × 11-inch pan. Cover with date filling.

Date Filling:

2 cups chopped pitted dates	1 cup water
1 cup brown sugar	1 tablespoon lemon juice

Combine and boil till thick, about 8 to 10 minutes. Spread over bottom layer of dough. Cover with second half of dough. Bake at 325 degrees 1 hour. Cut into squares. *3 dozen*

Meringue Jam Bars [FANCY]

Three-layer pastry-like treat

2 cups sifted all-purpose flour	3 egg yolks
½ teaspoon baking powder	¼ cup water
¼ teaspoon salt	1 teaspoon vanilla
½ cup butter	1½ cups tart jam or marmalade
¼ cup sugar	

Sift together flour, baking powder and salt. Cream butter. Add sugar gradually. Beat in egg yolks one at a time. Add flour mixture alternately with water. Add vanilla. Press dough into 9 × 12-inch pan. Spread with jam. Cover with following meringue:

Meringue:

3 egg whites	1 cup chopped nuts
½ cup sugar	¼ teaspoon salt

Beat egg whites until stiff. Add sugar gradually. Fold in nuts. Spread over jam. Bake at 350 degrees 20 to 25 minutes. Cut into squares when cold. *4 dozen*

Meringue Nut Bars [FANCY]

Pretty and not so rich as most layered bars

Bottom Layer:

1½ cups sifted cake flour	1 cup granulated sugar
½ teaspoon salt	2 eggs, beaten
1 teaspoon baking powder	½ teaspoon vanilla
½ cup butter or margarine	

Sift together flour, salt and baking powder. Cream butter and sugar until fluffy. Add eggs, vanilla and sifted dry ingredients, mixing well. Spread in 9-inch-square pan. Cover with topping.

Topping:

1 egg white	1 cup chopped nuts
1 cup sifted brown sugar	

Beat egg white until stiff. Fold in brown sugar and nuts. Spread over dough. Bake at 325 degrees 30 minutes. Cut into squares. *3 dozen*

Mocha Nut Bars [FANCY]

A brownie-like bottom layer with coffee-flavored meringue top layer

Bottom Layer:

½ cup butter or margarine
1 cup sugar
2 eggs
1 teaspoon vanilla
1½ cups sifted all-purpose flour

½ teaspoon salt
1 teaspoon baking powder
2 ounces or squares unsweetened chocolate, melted

Cream butter and sugar well. Add eggs, then vanilla. Sift together dry ingredients and stir in. Add chocolate. Spread in 13 × 15-inch jelly roll pan. Cover with topping.

Topping:

1 egg white
1 cup brown sugar
1 teaspoon instant coffee

½ cup chopped nuts
½ cup flaked coconut

Beat egg white until stiff. Fold in brown sugar, instant coffee, nuts and coconut. Spread over dough. Bake at 325 degrees 30 to 35 minutes. Cut into squares when cool.
4 dozen

DROP COOKIES

Almond Kisses [FANCY]

As glamorous and shimmering as a movie star at a premiere

5 egg whites
2½ cups sifted powdered
   sugar
½ teaspoon salt

2 cups finely ground
   blanched almonds (or
   filberts)
1 teaspoon cinnamon

Beat egg whites until stiff. Sift powdered sugar and salt. Fold gently into egg whites. Fold in nuts and cinnamon. Drop on greased cookie sheet. Bake at 300 degrees 20 to 25 minutes, until firm. *About 6 dozen*

Brown Sugar Kisses [FANCY]

Delicate nutty meringue-type cookie

1 cup brown sugar, firmly
   packed
2 egg whites, beaten stiff
¼ teaspoon salt

3 tablespoons flour
1 teaspoon vanilla
1 cup finely ground pecans
   or filberts

Gradually beat brown sugar into beaten egg whites. Fold in flour, vanilla and nuts. Drop onto well-greased baking sheet. Bake at 350 degrees about 10 minutes. *4 dozen*

Cherry Coconut Balls [FANCY]

Chewy and colorful

1 cup sugar
¾ cup butter or margarine
1 egg
1 teaspoon vanilla
2 cups sifted all-purpose
 flour
½ teaspoon baking powder

½ teaspoon salt
½ cup chopped maraschino
 cherries
½ cup snipped grated
 coconut
½ cup chopped nuts

Cream shortening and sugar. Blend in egg and vanilla. Sift together dry ingredients and add. Then add cherries, coconut and nuts. Drop onto lightly greased baking sheet. Bake at 375 degrees about 10 minutes. When cool, spread with Pink Fondant Glaze. *4 dozen*

Pink Fondant Glaze:

1½ cups sifted powdered
 sugar

2 tablespoons maraschino
 cherry juice
¼ teaspoon salt

Blend well and spread on cooled cookies.

Lace Cookies [FANCY]

Fragile and delicious, rolled or not

½ cup butter
¾ cup sugar
¼ cup honey or light corn
 syrup

1 cup sifted all-purpose
 flour
½ teaspoon nutmeg
½ teaspoon brandy
 flavoring

Cream butter. Blend in sugar. Add honey. Stir in flour and flavorings. Drop well apart on ungreased cookie sheet. Bake at 375 degrees about 8 minutes. Let cool 2 or 3 minutes, then remove to rack gently. If desired, roll while hot around wooden spoon handle. If cookies become too brittle to roll or to remove from baking sheet, return to hot oven for a minute or two. *About 6 dozen*

Lemon Chips [PLAIN]

Crisp and flavored with fresh lemon

½ cup butter or margarine
1 cup sugar
1 egg
3 tablespoons lemon juice
2 teaspoons grated lemon rind

2 cups sifted all-purpose flour
1 teaspoon baking powder
½ teaspoon baking soda
½ teaspoon salt
½ cup flaked coconut
½ cup chopped nuts

Cream butter and sugar. Beat in egg, lemon juice and rind. Sift together dry ingredients and add. Stir in coconut and nuts. Drop onto lightly greased baking sheet. Bake at 375 degrees 10 to 12 minutes. *4 dozen*

Macaroons [PLAIN]

A chewy coconut version

3 egg whites
⅔ cup sugar
3 tablespoons flour

¼ teaspoon salt
2 cups grated coconut
1 teaspoon vanilla

Beat egg whites till stiff, gradually beating in sugar. Fold in sifted flour and salt, coconut and vanilla. Drop on lightly greased baking sheet. Bake at 325 degrees 15 to 20 minutes. *3 dozen*

Maple Sugar Crisps [FANCY]

Unusual and very good

2 egg whites
1 cup shaved maple sugar
1 cup chopped nuts

1 cup coarse graham
  cracker crumbs
¼ teaspoon salt

Beat egg whites until stiff. Beat in sugar. Fold in nuts, cracker crumbs and salt. Drop on lightly greased baking sheet. Bake at 325 degrees 15 minutes. *3 dozen*

Oatmeal Coconut Cherry Crisps [FANCY]

Wonderfully chewy and colorful

¾ cup butter or margarine
1½ cups light brown sugar,
  firmly packed
2 eggs
1 cup flaked coconut
¾ cup rolled oats
½ cup finely chopped
  walnuts

½ cup finely chopped maraschino cherries
1½ teaspoons vanilla
1 cup sifted flour
½ teaspoon baking soda
½ teaspoon salt

Cream butter until fluffy and gradually beat in sugar. Stir in eggs, coconut, oats, walnuts, cherries and vanilla, blending well. Sift together dry ingredients and add. Drop on lightly greased cookie sheet. Bake at 325 degrees 10 minutes. *4 dozen*

Orange Buttermilk Frosted Cookies [FANCY]

Old-fashioned buttermilk and lard-tender cookies

2 cups sugar	5 cups sifted all-purpose
1 cup lard (or use ½ cup	flour
shortening and ½ cup	1 teaspoon baking soda
butter)	1 cup buttermilk
2 eggs	3 tablespoons orange juice
1 teaspoon salt	2 teaspoons grated orange
	rind

Cream sugar and lard until fluffy. Add beaten eggs. Sift together flour and salt. Dissolve soda in buttermilk. Add alternately to lard mixture with dry ingredients. Add orange rind and juice. Drop by teaspoonfuls onto lightly greased baking sheet. Bake at 400 degrees 10 minutes. Cool, then frost with Orange Icing. *7 dozen*

Orange Icing:

2 tablespoons melted butter	About 1½ cups powdered
Juice and grated rind of 1	sugar
orange	

Blend butter, orange juice and rind with enough sugar for good spreading consistency. Ice cookies thinly. Double recipe if you wish a thick layer of icing.

Pecan Crisps [PLAIN]

Rich and tender-crisp

½ cup butter	1 cup sifted cake flour
2 tablespoons sugar	1 cup pecans, finely
1 teaspoon vanilla	chopped

Beat butter until soft. Add sugar and blend until creamy. Add vanilla, then sifted flour and nuts. Work with hands to form dough. Drop onto ungreased baking sheet. Bake at 300 degrees about 25 minutes or until firm but not brown. *About 2½ dozen*

Pecan Macaroons [PLAIN]

Pecans give these an inimitable flavor

4 egg whites
1 cup sugar

1 teaspoon vanilla
1 cup pecans, ground very fine

Beat egg whites until stiff. Add sugar gradually, continuing to beat. Add vanilla and nuts. Drop on greased baking sheet. Bake at 225 degrees 45 minutes. *3 dozen*

Pineapple Macaroons [FANCY]

Flavorful, fruited macaroons that are deliciously chewy

3 egg whites
¼ teaspoon salt
1 cup sugar
1 teaspoon grated lemon rind

½ cup well-drained pineapple
2 cups grated coconut

Beat egg whites until stiff. Add salt, then sugar gradually, continuing to beat. Add lemon rind, pineapple and coconut. Drop on greased baking sheet. Bake at 325 degrees about 20 minutes. *3 dozen*

Rice Flour Almondettes [FANCY]

Crisp, fragile and dainty

3 eggs	½ teaspoon almond extract
1 cup sugar	½ cup blanched, slivered
1 cup sifted rice flour	almonds
¼ teaspoon salt	

Beat eggs and sugar together until very thick and light. Fold in rice flour, salt, almond extract and nuts. Drop by teaspoonfuls onto lightly greased baking sheet. Bake at 350 degrees about 15 minutes. *3 dozen*

Sesame Brown Sugar Drops [FANCY]

Chewy and richly flavored

1 cup sesame seed	¾ cup sifted all-purpose
⅓ cup water	flour
1 cup brown sugar	¼ teaspoon salt
¼ cup melted butter	1 egg

Cook sesame seed in water over low heat until water is nearly absorbed. Combine with brown sugar and melted butter. Add the flour and salt. Stir in beaten egg. Drop on ungreased baking sheet. Bake at 350 degrees 10 to 12 minutes. *2 dozen*

FILLED COOKIES

Date-filled Rolled Cookies [FANCY]

Enhanced with orange and honey

1 cup shortening	3 teaspoons baking powder
1 cup brown sugar	1¼ teaspoons salt
1 cup honey	6½ cups sifted all-purpose
2 eggs	flour
1½ teaspoons vanilla	Date Orange Filling
1 tablespoon grated orange rind	

Blend soft shortening with sugar and honey. Add beaten eggs, vanilla and orange rind. Sift together dry ingredients and add in three parts. Chill dough 2 hours. Roll a small portion of dough at a time on lightly floured board. Cut into rounds. Place ½ teaspoon Date Orange Filling in center. Top with another round of cookie dough which has been cut into a decorative pattern, if desired. Cut a small jack-o'-lantern face at Halloween or use tiny cutters such as stars, trees and so on to remove center of top round. An alternate cutting method is simply to crisscross slash in center of dough. Press edges together with fork tines. Lay on lightly greased baking sheet. Bake at 400 degrees about 15 minutes. *About 5 dozen*

Date Orange Filling:

2 cups chopped pitted dates	¼ cup water
½ cup sugar	2 teaspoons grated orange
½ cup orange juice	rind

Combine dates, sugar, orange juice and water. Cook and stir until thick. Add grated orange rind. Cool.

Mocha-filled Cookies [FANCY]

Rich chocolate- and coffee-flavored filling

1 recipe dough for Basic Sugar Cookies (see index)
Mocha Filling

Prepare dough according to recipe. Roll on lightly floured board. Cut 3½-inch rounds. Place spoonful of Mocha Filling in center. Fold dough over filling, piercing top with fork tines or making two small slits with sharp-pointed knife. Seal edges by pressing with floured fork tines or fingertips. Bake on ungreased cookie sheets at 400 degrees about 12 minutes or until golden brown. *About 3 dozen*

Mocha Filling:

¼ cup fine dry bread crumbs
½ cup sugar
3 tablespoons melted butter

1 ounce or square unsweetened chocolate, melted
2 teaspoons instant coffee

Stir crumbs and sugar together. Then mix in melted butter, chocolate and coffee powder.

Phoebe's Fig-filled Cookies [FANCY]

Tender lemon-flavored dough with creamy fig filling

½ cup butter
1 cup sugar
1 egg
1 tablespoon lemon juice
Grated rind of 1 lemon
½ teaspoon baking soda

½ teaspoon salt
3 cups sifted all-purpose flour
½ cup buttermilk or sour milk
Fig Filling

Cream butter and sugar. Add beaten egg, lemon juice and grated rind. Sift together dry ingredients and add alternately with buttermilk or sour milk. Chill 1 hour. Roll dough thin on lightly floured board. Cut into rounds. Place 1 teaspoonful Fig Filling between two rounds of cookie dough. Seal edges by pressing lightly with floured fork tines or fingertips. Bake on ungreased cookie sheet at 375 degrees about 15 minutes. *About 5 dozen*

Fig Filling:

1 cup chopped figs (ground raisins, dates or a combination of dry fruits may be used)

2 salted crackers, rolled fine

Juice and grated rind of 1 lemon

½ cup sugar

1 egg

Combine ingredients and cook over low heat, stirring constantly, until thick. Cool.

Thimble Tarts [FANCY]

1 recipe dough for Basic Sugar Cookies (see index)
1 cup fruit jam

Prepare plain rolled dough according to recipe. Cut in 2-inch rounds. With thimble remove center from half of rounds. (If large cookie cutter is used—3-inch diameter or over—three small circles may be cut in half the rounds.) Spread plain rounds with jam and top with cut-out rounds. If desired, small slits may be made in top rounds instead of removing part of dough with thimble-cutter. Bake filled cookies according to basic recipe directions, avoiding overbrowning. The quantity of double cookies will be about half that of single cookies.

ICEBOX COOKIES

Almond Wafers [PLAIN]

Buttery-rich, delicate cookie

½ cup butter
½ cup sugar
2 egg yolks
½ teaspoon almond extract
¼ teaspoon vanilla

1 cup sifted all-purpose
flour
⅔ cup whole unblanched
almonds, measured and
then ground very fine

Cream butter until soft, blend in sugar. Add egg yolks and flavorings. Beat batter until smooth. Mix ground almonds with flour and gradually stir into butter mixture. Form in rolls. Wrap in waxed paper or aluminum foil. Chill 6 to 8 hours. Slice thin. Bake on lightly greased sheet at 400 degrees 8 to 10 minutes. *3 to 4 dozen*

Spiced Almond Wafers [PLAIN]

Delicately spiced version

1 recipe dough for Almond
Wafers

1 teaspoon cinnamon
¼ teaspoon nutmeg

Prepare dough as directed for Almond Wafers, sifting spices with flour before mixing with ground nuts. Chill, slice and bake as directed above.

Anise Crisps [PLAIN]

Both oatmeal and anise give these distinction

1 cup butter or margarine
1 cup sugar
1 egg
½ teaspoon vanilla
½ teaspoon ground anise or
1 tablespoon crushed
anise seed

½ teaspoon salt
½ teaspoon baking powder
2 cups sifted all-purpose
flour
1½ cups rolled oats

Beat butter or margarine until very soft. Blend in sugar gradually. Add slightly beaten egg, vanilla and anise powder or seed. Sift together salt, baking powder and flour and add in three portions. Work in rolled oats in two additions to make a stiff dough. Form into rolls. Wrap in waxed paper or aluminum foil. Chill 6 to 8 hours. Slice ¼ inch thick. Bake on ungreased cookie sheet at 400 degrees 10 minutes. *About 5 dozen*

Black Walnut Fingers [PLAIN]

Show off all the goodness of black walnuts

¾ cup butter
2 cups brown sugar, firmly
packed
2 eggs
2 teaspoons vanilla
3 cups sifted all-purpose
flour

1½ teaspoons baking
powder
¼ teaspoon salt
½ cup black walnuts, finely
chopped

Cream butter and sugar. Add well-beaten eggs and vanilla. Sift together dry ingredients and stir in. Add nuts. Form into rolls. Wrap in waxed paper or aluminum foil. Chill 6 to 8 hours. Slice thin. Bake on ungreased sheet at 425 degrees 6 to 8 minutes. *5 to 6 dozen*

Chocolate Mint Icebox Cookies [FANCY]

Crisp chocolate cookies with mint filling

½ cup shortening	2 cups sifted all-purpose
¾ cup sugar	flour
1 egg	1 teaspoon baking powder
1 teaspoon vanilla	½ teaspoon salt
½ cup ground chocolate	Mint Filling
2 tablespoons hot milk	

Blend sugar into soft shortening gradually. Beat in egg and vanilla well. Stir chocolate into hot milk, then add to mixture. Sift together dry ingredients and add in three portions, blending thoroughly. Chill 3 hours. Slice thin. Bake on lightly greased sheet at 375 degrees 6 to 8 minutes. Cool. Spread 1 round with Mint Filling and top with another round. *4 dozen small double cookies*

Mint Filling:

3 tablespoons butter	4 to 6 drops mint extract
1¾ cups sifted powdered	Green food coloring, if
sugar	desired
2 tablespoons hot cream	

Blend sifted powdered sugar into soft butter, adding cream and mint flavoring. Taste and add additional mint extract, if desired, but avoid too strong a flavoring. Tint as desired with green food coloring.

Cinnamon Chocolate Thins [FANCY]

A wonderful flavor combination in a rich, crisp cookie

½ cup butter
1 cup sugar
1 egg
1¼ teaspoons vanilla
2 ounces or squares
  unsweetened chocolate
2¼ cups sifted all-purpose
  flour

1 teaspoon baking powder
¼ teaspoon salt
¾ teaspoon cinnamon
3 tablespoons cream
Pecans for garnish, if
  desired

Cream butter and sugar until light. Add slightly beaten egg, vanilla and melted, cooled chocolate. Sift together dry ingredients and add alternately with cream. Shape into rolls. Wrap in waxed paper or aluminum foil. Chill 6 to 8 hours. Slice thin. Bake on lightly greased cookie sheet. Top with whole pecans, if desired. Bake at 400 degrees 5 to 7 minutes. *About 4 dozen*

Lemon Bars [PLAIN]

Crisp and as refreshingly flavored as lemonade

½ cup butter or margarine
½ cup shortening
1 cup brown sugar, firmly
  packed
1 cup white sugar
2 eggs
1 tablespoon lemon juice

2 teaspoons grated lemon
  rind
1 teaspoon vanilla
3¼ cups sifted all-purpose
  flour
2 teaspoons baking powder
½ teaspoon salt

Cream butter or margarine and shortening together until soft and well mixed. Gradually add sugars. Add slightly beaten eggs, lemon juice, grated lemon rind and vanilla. Beat until smooth. Sift together dry ingredients and stir in. Chill overnight in rolls wrapped in waxed paper or aluminum foil. Slice thin. Bake on ungreased sheet at 400 degrees 10 minutes. *6 to 7 dozen*

Orange Nut Slices [PLAIN]

Delicately flavored with orange, crisp with nuts

1 cup butter
½ cup white sugar
½ cup brown sugar, firmly packed
1 egg
4 teaspoons grated orange rind

2½ cups sifted all-purpose flour
½ teaspoon baking powder
¼ teaspoon salt
⅔ cup finely chopped nuts (almonds, filberts, pecans or walnuts)
2 tablespoons orange juice

Cream butter until soft, add sugars gradually, blending well. Stir in slightly beaten egg and grated orange rind. Sift together flour, baking powder and salt. Add finely chopped nuts to flour mixture. Stir in flour-nut mixture alternately with orange juice. Shape dough in rolls. Wrap in waxed paper or aluminum foil. Chill 6 to 8 hours. Slice thin. Bake on ungreased cookie sheet at 400 degrees 8 to 10 minutes. *About 5 dozen*

NO-BAKE COOKIES

No-bake Dream Bars [FANCY]

A quick, delicious, rich version of that popular cookie

12 double graham crackers	1 cup quartered maraschino
½ cup melted butter	cherries
1 cup sugar	1 cup chopped nuts
½ cup milk	1 cup coarse graham
2 eggs, beaten	cracker crumbs
1 cup grated coconut	

Arrange 6 whole graham crackers in bottom of 9 × 13-inch pan, covering entire pan. Combine melted butter, sugar, milk and eggs. Bring to boil, stirring constantly. Remove from heat and add remaining ingredients. Pour over graham crackers. Press remaining double graham crackers in place, covering entire top. Cool, then refrigerate until ready to serve. Cut in squares. *4 dozen*

Quick Unbaked Brownies [PLAIN]

A rich, chewy, fudgelike treat

1 cup undiluted evaporated milk	1 cup sugar
	¼ teaspoon salt
32 marshmallows, quartered, or 3 cups miniatures	3½ cups fine vanilla wafer or graham cracker crumbs
3 squares or ounces unsweetened chocolate, melted	1 cup chopped nuts

Combine evaporated milk, marshmallows, chocolate, sugar

and salt. Cook and stir over medium heat, bringing to full, all-over boil. Boil and stir 5 minutes more. Remove from heat and stir in crumbs and nuts. Spread in buttered 9-inch-square pan. Chill until firm. Cut into squares with knife dipped in hot water. Sprinkle with powdered sugar, if desired. *2 dozen*

PRESSED COOKIES

Cream Cheese Almond Bars [FANCY]

Very rich, delicate dough, but easily handled

1 cup butter	¼ teaspoon vanilla
1 3-ounce package cream cheese	2 cups sifted all-purpose flour
½ cup sugar	1 cup ground almonds
½ teaspoon almond extract	

Cream room-temperature butter and cream cheese together until well blended. Stir in sugar thoroughly. Add flavorings. Add flour in three portions, mixing well after all is added. Form bar cookies with cookie press on ungreased cookie sheet. Sprinkle with finely ground nuts. Bake at 375 degrees 8 to 10 minutes. *4 dozen*

Wreath Cookies [FANCY]

Same dough, different shape!

Use above dough with star plate to form tiny wreaths, pressing ends of dough together with fingertips. Omit nuts. Bake at 375 degrees 8 to 10 minutes. *4 dozen*

Lemon Wafers [FANCY]

Very crisp, with delicate lemon flavoring and gently sweetened

¾ cup shortening
6 tablespoons powdered sugar
2 tablespoons lemon juice
½ teaspoon grated lemon rind

1 teaspoon vanilla
1½ cups sifted all-purpose flour
¼ teaspoon salt
Colored decorating sugars

Cream shortening until soft. Add powdered sugar gradually. Beat in lemon juice, grated rind and vanilla. Sift together flour and salt and add gradually, blending well after each addition. Put dough through cookie press on ungreased baking sheet. Decorate with colored sugars, if desired. Bake at 400 degrees 8 to 10 minutes. *3 dozen*

ROLLED COOKIES

Almond Cream Sandwiches [FANCY]

Pastry-like cookies with creamy, almond-flavored filling

1 cup butter
5 tablespoons whipping cream

2 cups sifted all-purpose flour
Almond Cream Filling

Beat butter until very light, then stir in flour alternately with cream. Chill dough 1 hour. Roll very thin on lightly floured board, then cut in rounds with small floured cutter. Lay on ungreased baking sheet and sprinkle cookies generously with granulated sugar. (A salt shaker reserved for just this use is a real aid to a confirmed cookie-maker.) Pierce dough with fork in 2 or 3 places. Bake at 400 degrees 5 to 7 minutes. Cool. Put two cookies together sandwich-style with Almond Cream Filling.

Almond Cream Filling:

3 tablespoons butter
⅔ cup sifted powdered
   sugar

1 egg yolk
½ teaspoon almond extract
¼ teaspoon vanilla

Cream butter until soft, then stir in remaining ingredients. Divide cream filling into three containers. Tint with food coloring for a pale yellow, delicate pink and light green. Dip toothpick into food coloring and then into filling. Mix well and add additional coloring the same way, if needed. *About 3 dozen*

Almond Paste-topped Butter Cookies [FANCY]

Crisp butter cookies with baked-on almond topping

1 cup butter
1 cup sugar
1 egg or 2 egg yolks, beaten
½ teaspoon salt

¼ teaspoon baking powder
2 cups sifted all-purpose
   flour
Almond Paste Topping

Cream butter well. Blend in sugar, then beaten egg. Sift together dry ingredients and add. Chill dough 1 hour. Roll out thin on lightly floured board. Cut with floured round or scalloped cutter 2 inches in diameter. Place on ungreased cookie sheet and return to refrigerator while preparing topping.

Almond Paste Topping:

3 cups (½ pound) blanched
   almonds, very finely
   ground

1¾ cups sifted powdered
   sugar
¼ teaspoon almond extract
Water to moisten

Stir ground almonds into sugar, then add almond extract and a few drops of water gradually, to make a thick paste which may be rolled on waxed paper dusted lightly with powdered sugar. Cut 1½-inch rounds to lay on top of each 2-inch butter cookie. Bake at 400 degrees 8 to 10 minutes. *4 dozen*

Brazilian Treats [PLAIN]

Deliciously flavored with coffee and cinnamon-sugar-glazed

⅔ cup shortening	3 cups sifted all-purpose
1 cup sugar	flour
2 eggs	2 teaspoons instant coffee
1 teaspoon vanilla	¼ cup boiling water
1 teaspoon salt	¼ cup sugar, additional
1½ teaspoons baking	1 teaspoon cinnamon
powder	

Cream shortening. Add sugar and blend until lightly fluffy. Beat in eggs, one at a time, blending first completely before second egg is added. Add vanilla. Sift together dry ingredients. Dissolve coffee in hot water. Add dry ingredients alternately with hot coffee. Chill dough 2 hours. Roll on lightly floured board and cut with floured cutters into rounds, squares or fancy shapes. Mix ¼ cup sugar with the cinnamon and sprinkle over cookies after they are arranged on ungreased baking sheet. Bake at 400 degrees 10 to 12 minutes. *About 6 dozen*

Chocolate Scallops [FANCY]

Delicious filled cookie that's easily done with chocolate mints

    1 recipe Basic Sugar Cookie dough (see index)
    1 7-ounce package chocolate mint wafers (the hard, flat kind, not creams)

Roll dough to ⅛-inch thickness on lightly floured board. Cut into 2-inch scalloped rounds. Lay on cookie sheet. Top each round with thin chocolate mint wafer. Bake at 375 degrees 8 minutes or until chocolate is melted, but not scorched or bubbled, and cookies are lightly golden in color. Remove to wire racks and let stand until chocolate solidifies (this may take several hours). *3 dozen* (Bake excess dough in plain rounds sprinkled with sugar.)

Circus Mint Cookies [FANCY]

Sugar cookies topped with striped candy mints

1 recipe Basic Sugar Cookie dough (see index)

1 package 1-inch-diameter red and white striped candy mints

Roll cookie dough to ¼-inch thickness on lightly floured board. Cut into rounds with 1¼-inch cutter. Lay on baking sheet and top each with a red and white candy mint. Bake at 375 degrees about 10 minutes. Avoid overbaking so that mint stays whole and unchanged in color. *4 dozen or more*

Cookie Napoleons [FANCY]

Three-layer creations that look elaborate, taste delicious but aren't hard to do

1 recipe Basic Rolled Sugar Cookie dough (see index)
1 recipe Chocolate Glaze and Filling (see below)

1 recipe White Glaze (optional) (see below)
Nuts or candied cherries for decoration

Prepare dough according to directions. Roll out ⅛ inch thick on lightly floured board. Cut into rectangles, 3 × 1½ inches, with knife or pastry wheel. Bake on ungreased sheet at 375 degrees 8 to 10 minutes. Cool. Prepare fillings.

Chocolate Glaze and Filling:

1 tablespoon flour
¼ cup sugar
Few grains salt
½ cup milk

1 8-ounce package semi-sweet chocolate bits
½ teaspoon vanilla
½ cup whipping cream

Combine flour, sugar and salt. Gradually stir in cold milk. Bring to boil over low heat, stirring constantly. Remove from heat. Add chocolate bits and vanilla, stirring until chocolate melts. Spread on a third of the cooled cookies. Allow remainder of chocolate filling to cool. Beat cream until stiff, then fold into cooled chocolate mixture. Chill. Spread on remaining cookies. Stack two cookies covered with chocolate-whipped cream mixture together, then top with glazed chocolate cookie, which may be decorated with slivered almonds, finely chopped pecans or other nut meats or with candied cherries.

Optional White Glaze:

¾ cup sifted powdered sugar
¼ teaspoon vanilla

About 1 tablespoon hot water

Add vanilla and water to powdered sugar to make a thin glaze. Spread over one third of the cookies which are to be glazed, if desired, decorating white glaze with chocolate glaze put through decorating tube, or with candied fruits or nut meats. White glaze may be tinted with food coloring, too, to create special decorative effects. *16 to 18 3-layer cookies*

Filled Butter Rings [FANCY]

Doughnut-shaped top cookie layer lets the filling peek through

1 recipe Basic Rolled Sugar	1 recipe Vanilla, Lemon or
Cookie dough (see index)	Orange Filling

Divide dough in half. Roll one portion on lightly floured board to ⅛-inch thickness. Cut with round cookie cutter. Roll remaining portion of dough and cut with round cookie cutter with hole in center (doughnut cutter). Place cookies—plain and doughnut-shaped—on ungreased cookie sheet. Bake according to recipe directions. Cool. Fill with either Vanilla, Orange or Lemon Filling.

Vanilla Filling:

⅓ cup flour	2 eggs
⅔ cup sugar	1 tablespoon butter
¼ teaspoon salt	1 teaspoon vanilla
2 cups scalded milk	Glazed cherries for garnish

Mix flour, sugar and salt. Stir in scalded milk gradually. Cook and stir over very low heat or in double boiler until thickened, stirring constantly. Add a portion of hot mixture to slightly beaten eggs, then return eggs to remaining hot mixture, stirring constantly. Add butter and cook and stir until eggs thicken, about 3 to 5 minutes. Cool. Add vanilla.

Spread plain rounds with cooled filling, top with doughnut-shaped ring. Garnish with bit of glazed cherry in center, if desired. *About 2 dozen*

Lemon Filling:

¼ cup flour	⅔ cup water
¾ cup sugar	1 egg
⅛ teaspoon salt	1 tablespoon butter
Juice and grated rind of 1 lemon	

Mix flour, sugar and salt. Stir in lemon juice and grated rind, water and slightly beaten egg. Cook and stir over very low heat or over boiling water until thickened, about 8 to 10 minutes. Add butter, stir to blend. Cool. Fill as above.

Orange Filling:

3 tablespoons flour	1 egg
½ cup sugar	1 tablespoon grated orange
⅛ teaspoon salt	rind
2 tablespoons lemon juice	1 tablespoon butter
½ cup orange juice	

Mix flour, sugar and salt. Stir in lemon and orange juices, slightly beaten egg and grated orange rind. Cook and stir over very low heat or boiling water until thickened, about 8 to 10 minutes. Add butter. Stir to blend. Cool. Fill as directed above.

Filled Silhouette Cookies [FANCY]

Cookie sandwiches with cream filling, "silhouetted" in top cookie design cutout

    1 recipe Basic Rolled Sugar Cookie dough (see index)
    Butter Cream Icing
    Colored decorating sugars

Divide rolled dough in half. Roll one portion on lightly floured board to ⅛-inch thickness. Cut with round cutter. Prepare remaining dough in same manner. From these rounds, remove centers with tiny cutters in special shapes: animals, trees, stars or Christmas ornaments. Bake all cookies on baking sheet according to recipe. Cool. Spread entire surface of whole rounds with Butter Cream Icing. Top with silhouette cookies. Fill opening with light sprinkling of colored decorating sugar.

Butter Cream Icing:

3 tablespoons butter	1 teaspoon vanilla
2 cups sifted powdered sugar	2 tablespoons cream

Cream butter until soft. Gradually stir in powdered sugar, vanilla and cream, blending until smooth. Add additional powdered sugar, if necessary, for good spreading consistency. Too soft an icing makes a hard-to-handle cookie. *About 3 dozen filled cookies*

Ice Cream Cookie Cups [FANCY]

Thin, crisp cups to fill with ice cream

1⅓ cups sifted powdered sugar	1 cup butter
¼ teaspoon salt	1 egg, beaten
2½ cups sifted all-purpose flour	2 teaspoons vanilla

Sift sugar, salt and flour into mixing bowl. Cut in butter. Combine egg and vanilla, then add to flour mixture a small amount at a time, mixing lightly but thoroughly. Chill 2 hours. Roll dough thin on lightly floured board and cut in 5-inch circles. Form over backs of muffin cups, trimming edges carefully. Place in 350-degree oven and bake 8 to 10 minutes until lightly browned. Cool, but remove from cups before completely cold. Serve filled with scoop of ice cream. *8 cups*

Jelly-filled Rings [FANCY]

Cookies, crisp and delicious, sandwiched together like a jelly doughnut

1 recipe Basic Rolled Sugar Cookie dough (see index)	1 cup currant, raspberry or other red jelly Powdered sugar

Divide rolled dough in half. Roll one portion on lightly floured board to ¼-inch thickness. Cut into rounds with scalloped cutter. Prepare second portion of dough in same fashion, using a small plain cutter to remove a center round of dough. Place rounds and rings on cookie sheet and bake as cookie recipe directs. Cool. Place a spoonful of jelly in center of round cookie. Dust doughnut-shaped rings with powdered sugar, then place on top of jelly-filled rounds. *About 2 dozen*

Macaroon-topped Butter Cookies [FANCY]

Macaroon-like meringue caps on crisp butter cookies

1 cup butter	½ teaspoon vanilla
1 cup sugar	3 cups sifted all-purpose
3 egg yolks	flour
1 egg white	1 teaspoon baking powder
½ teaspoon almond extract	½ teaspoon salt

Cream butter well, then blend in sugar, slightly beaten egg yolks and white and flavorings. Sift together dry ingredients and add. Chill dough 2 hours. Roll thin on lightly floured board and cut into rounds with floured cutter. Place on ungreased cookie sheet. Chill while preparing topping.

Macaroon Topping:

2 egg whites
¾ cup sugar

1¼ cups (¼ pound) al-
monds, very finely ground
2 drops almond extract

Beat egg whites until stiff peaks form, then gradually beat in sugar, continuing to beat until no graininess may be felt when batter is pinched between thumb and forefinger. Add vanilla. Fold in almonds. Top each butter cookie with a bit of meringue. Bake at 375 degrees until lightly browned and meringue is cooked through, about 10 to 12 minutes. *6 dozen*

Minted Chocolate Wafers [FANCY]

Crisp chocolate cookies with mint-flavored filling

1 recipe rolled Chocolate Dollars (see index)
Mint Cream Filling

Prepare Chocolate Dollars according to recipe directions. Cut into 1½-inch rounds. Bake as directed. Cool and make sandwich-like cookies with Mint Cream Filling.

Mint Cream Filling: Prepare Butter Cream Icing (see index) reducing vanilla to ¼ teaspoon and adding ⅛ teaspoon mint extract. Blend and taste. Add additional mint, if desired, but be careful not to make flavoring too dominant. Tint delicate green, if desired. *2 dozen "sandwiches"*

Orange Cream Sandwiches [FANCY]

Orange flavoring in the dough, orange flavoring in filling

1 recipe dough for Punch Bowl Cookies (see index)
Orange Cream Filling

Flavor dough with 1 tablespoon orange juice in place of

vanilla or lemon extract. Use 1 teaspoon grated orange rind instead of both lemon and orange rind. Roll out small portions of chilled dough on floured board and cut into small rounds—about 1½ inches in diameter. Omit glaze. Bake as directed. Cool. Put two cookies together with Orange Cream Filling.

Orange Cream Filling:

3 tablespoons soft butter	1 teaspoon grated orange rind
2 cups sifted powdered sugar	3 tablespoons orange juice

Cream butter. Add powdered sugar, grated rind and orange juice gradually, blending until smooth. Add additional sugar, if needed, for good spreading consistency.

Picture Cookies [FANCY]

Chocolate "press" cookies prettily outlined—and baked—on light butter cookies

1 recipe chocolate Spritz I or II dough (see index)	1 recipe Basic Rolled Sugar Cookie dough (see index)

Form small press cookies on an ungreased cookie sheet. Chill while rolling and cutting Sugar Cookie dough into rounds about 2¼ to 2½ inches in diameter. Place plain rounds on cookie sheet. Using spatula, carefully lay formed chocolate cookies on top of unbaked light dough rounds. Bake 10 to 12 minutes at 400 degrees. *About 3 dozen*

Punch Bowl Cookies [PLAIN]

Thin, crisp cookies, delicately flavored with orange and lemon rinds

1 cup butter
1 cup sugar
1 egg, unbeaten, or 2 yolks
1 teaspoon vanilla or ½ teaspoon lemon extract
½ teaspoon grated lemon rind
½ teaspoon grated orange rind

½ teaspoon salt
2 cups sifted all-purpose flour less 2 tablespoons
1 egg white to brush tops of cookies
Nutmeg or cinnamon or small bits of candied fruit or slivered almonds to garnish

Cream butter, stir in sugar and then egg or yolks. Add flavoring and grated rinds. Stir in sifted flour and salt. Chill covered dough 1 hour. Pinch off a small piece of dough to roll, returning remainder to refrigerator. Cut cookies in desired shapes. Brush tops with beaten egg white and decorate with bits of candied fruit or nuts or dust with nutmeg or cinnamon in place of fruit or nuts, if desired. Bake at 400 degrees 5 minutes on ungreased sheet. *4 dozen*

Rich Nut Sticks [PLAIN]

Full of nuts 'n' flavor—rich and crisp

1 cup butter or margarine
1 cup sugar
2 egg yolks
1 tablespoon sour cream
¼ teaspoon salt

1¼ cups finely ground almonds, walnuts, pecans, filberts or Brazil nuts
2 cups sifted all-purpose flour

Cream butter, add sugar gradually, creaming until well mixed. Add egg yolks, beating well. Combine salt, nut meats and flour. Add to butter mixture, blending until smooth, compact dough is formed. Roll dough on lightly floured board to ⅓-inch thickness. Cut in strips 3 × 1 inches. Place on cookie sheet. Prick top with fork tines. Bake at 350 degrees 12 to 15 minutes. *About 3 dozen*

Rich Rolled Cookies [PLAIN]

Very rich, golden-with-egg-yolks Danish delight

⅔ cup butter, margarine or shortening
1 cup sugar
3 hard-cooked egg yolks, sieved

4 raw egg yolks
1 teaspoon vanilla
2 cups sifted all-purpose flour
½ teaspoon salt

Cream butter, blend in sugar and sieved egg yolks. (Drop unbroken yolks into hot water and simmer until firm, then press through sieve while hot.) Mix raw yolks slightly with fork, then add to butter mixture with vanilla. Work in flour which has been sifted with salt, in about three parts. If dough is dry, add a few drops of cream. If dough is too soft to roll, knead in a little flour on board but keep additional flour at minimum to avoid toughening. Roll small amount of dough ¼ inch thick, covering remainder of dough with cloth which has been wrung out with cold water, to avoid drying out. Cut in desired shapes.

If glaze is desired, brush cookies with mixture of 1 egg white beaten slightly with 2 teaspoons water. Decorate with colored sugars, nuts or candied fruits.

Bake on ungreased cookie sheet at 400 degrees 8 to 10 minutes. Cool on rack. *3 to 4 dozen*

Christmas Cookie Baking Time

Mere mention of Christmas cookie baking may bring back such pleasurable memories that no additional word will be needed to set you forth on this annual activity. But just in case fruitcake and mincemeat have been your forte previously, let us say a bit for the less pretentious cookie!

Part of the joy of opening a prettily wrapped package of Christmas cookies (or being asked to partake of a platter of them) lies in the very contrast of the cookies included.

Rather than doubling or tripling a batch of dough to make large quantities of one variety, for Christmas cookies use small recipes and those as varied in flavor, color and texture as can be managed. An assortment may include decorated and frosted cookies from a basic rolled dough, a glazed cookie such as Lebkuchen, a plain or frosted bar, a version of layered cookies, fancy drops and a selection from the delicious unbaked ball cookies.

Cookies formed with a press from plain, chocolate or tinted dough delight the eye of the beholder. The pale goodness of Springerle formed with a beautifully carved board is a decorative sign of the season.

Flavor variety comes with a cookie rich in nut meats, fruit-filled or made with a hearty blend of molasses and spice. Filberts, Brazil nuts, black walnuts, cashews, blanched and

COOKIES IN
HOLIDAY DRESS

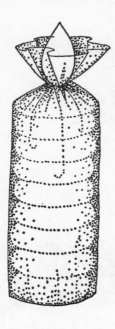

To make cookie candle, select and stack cookies of similar size and fairly flat—either rolled cookies or drop ones which bake flat. Wrap in cylinder in red cellophane and insert flame of gold foil.

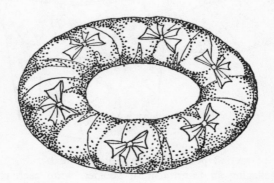

Cookie wreaths are easily and prettily made by overlapping cookies on circles of foil-covered cardboard, then overwrapping entire wreath with green cellophane. Bright bows of narrow red ribbon make gay "berries."

Just two of myriad possibilities suggested in text.

When packaging an assortment of cookies, wrap each cookie individually or in packets of two or three of same kind to keep flavors from mingling and soft cookies soft, and crisp ones crisp.

Use a variety of colored foils or other gay holiday papers that are oilproofed (or pre-wrap in wax paper). Let colors shine through clear plastic bag or gaily decorated jar.

unblanched almonds, pecans and pine nuts as well as such old reliables as English walnuts and peanuts are readily available to modern homemakers.

Unless you've worlds of time and patience, purchasing these in small packets ready for use is preferable to the troublesome chore of cracking, hulling, chopping and occasionally blanching. Where very perfect whole meats are desired for garnish, it may be necessary to begin with unshelled nuts. But check the local market supply first.

Make the most of colorful garnishes, using red and green candied cherries, golden pineapple, citron, candied peel, snowy coconut and tawny nut meats. Nature's storehouse of fruits is conveniently arrayed at every supermarket along with colorful decorating sugars—silver, yellow, green, red and those of mixed hue. Be sure to have a supply of food colors for tinting both doughs and frostings.

Use small, fancily shaped cutters for cookies of rolled dough—unless it's a gingerbread man you are making. Children adore them all sizes, but the larger the better.

For best results in Christmas cookie baking, first select the recipes to be used. Check the cupboard shelves for ingredients and add needed items to the shopping list. Don't overlook the fact that you may need extra sugar, probably three kinds: granulated, brown and powdered.

Choose a baking day free from other demanding tasks so that your entire attention can be focused on the mixing and baking. Most baking failures result from inaccurate measurement of ingredients caused by too hasty or careless attention to the recipe. Therefore, be calm and comfortably dressed with sufficient time to complete the baking successfully. Better to make one batch of cookies perfectly than produce several of questionable quality.

Christmas cookie baking is a creative pursuit akin in spirit to some of the higher arts, but happily one in which only a modest bit of talent is required. The rest depends on good kitchen practices, good ingredients and a serene point of view.

This is a time to let the children help and husbands, too, if so inclined. One husband whom we've heard about has developed quite a reputation for skillful frosting decorations and he and his wife send out to friends each year cookie packages that are eagerly anticipated for their toothsome and attractive contents.

Whatever type of container is used for presenting cookies as a gift, give a little thought to protecting the characteristic flavor and texture of each kind.

This may mean individual wrapping of each cookie when a single container holds both soft and crisp varieties. Or you may do a small "stack pack" with several of one kind wrapped together in a sheet of vaporproof packaging plastic developed for use in the freezer.

High points of color will result if you include some cookies wrapped in small pieces of colored foil, gold, red, green and patterned designs with a seasonal motif. Most everyone finds this kind of surprise intriguing—fine candy makers have been doing it for years.

Some cookies will not survive jostling and should be laid carefully on a rigid, flat surface for carrying. If necessary, construct a sturdy cardboard separator to hold one layer above another in a deep box. Make the separator like a lid—only sized to fit inside the box rather than over its top edges. Fill the first layer, placing cookies compactly with only sufficient room at each side to slip the lidlike separator into place. Then add a second layer, another separator and a third layer, if you wish.

A center crosswise support, or two of them placed at right

angles, may be required for protecting extremely delicate cookies or for use in widespread containers.

For very firm packaging, fill empty spaces with plain popped corn and gently shake container until a settled pack with no movement of the cookies is achieved. Suggestions for kinds of cookies to mail as well as packaging hints are in the chapter entitled "To Mail with Love."

One word of warning: be absolutely positive in selecting a container for a gift pack of cookies that there is no odor injurious to the flavor of the food about the container. Beauti-

PACKAGING FOR FRAGILE FANCY COOKIES

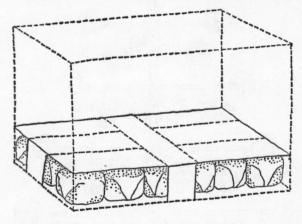

Wrap each cookie separately. Above each layer of cookies, place cardboard separator. If container is quite large, support separator with strips of cardboard.

ful boxes which have held perfumed soap, for example, never lose that scent and would make cookies packed in them—separately wrapped or not—inedible.

If you're a real expert at Christmas cookie making, perhaps you have collected gift containers for them all through the year. Because cookies come in many shapes and sizes, you can pack them in equally varied containers. Ball cookies in

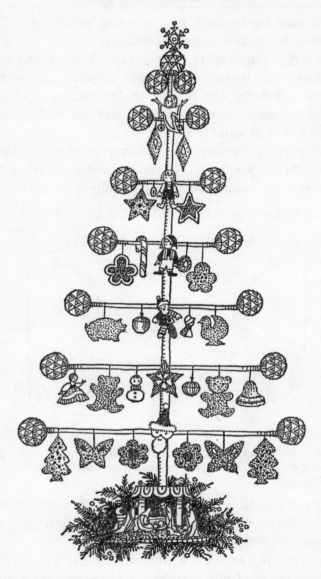

Gaily frosted and candy-decorated rolled cookies make this dowel tree a joy to behold. Red Swedish paper balls trim ends of "branches." Choose a variety of shapes from among the patterns given in this book

wide-mouth glass jars (it might be a peanut butter jar with a home-decorated lid), shortbread in metal canisters (buy these at a variety store), thin wafers overwrapped with foil in clear cellophane or plastic bags tied with ribbon are some of the possibilities.

New gift sacks or party bags fashioned just like those used by the corner grocery clerk, but in beautiful colors and satin-like paper, are both gay in appearance and easy to fill. Commercially available in large gift shops, the bags could readily be duplicated at home by persons quick with scissors and a pot of glue from roll gift-wrap paper, using a desired-size grocery bag as a pattern. Personalize these with names or adapt any of the hundreds of gala Christmas motifs for pretty packaging.

All kinds of boxes—from candy containers to thin stationery boxes—may serve for cookie gifts. These may be decorated with picture cookies—a Santa face, a gingerbread man or a tree with bright icing ornaments.

And baskets—what a wonderful assortment of these there is to choose from! Fat cornucopias, bread baskets, flat trays, miniature fishing creels, slender cracker baskets—these are a few.

Miniature trees—artificial or real—planted in a simple container are charming hung with tiny, decorated cookies. Such a gift is calculated to delight the heart of a child and equally pleasurable to some adults.

For party decorations, a cookie tree from which guests may partake is a fresh approach to refreshments. Ball cookies, for example, may be wrapped in colored transparent papers and tied onto the tree branches with glittering ribbons.

---

and from your own cutters. Hang carefully to achieve balanced effect. Smaller cookie trees for giving are delightful. For them, wrap cookies in a variety of colored cellophanes and tie on with ribbons.

Unwrapped, decorated cookies may be hung from tree branches, too, but preparation for this is done with raw dough. With great care, thread may sometimes be pulled through baked cookies—but too often the baked dough will crack or even shatter completely.

To prepare cookies for hanging on a tree, first lay the un-baked, cutout cookies rather widely separated on a prepared baking sheet. This allows thread run through the dough to rest on the sheet rather than fall over on another cookie and possibly bake fast to it.

Carefully pull a needle threaded with sturdy linen thread through each shape at a point of good balance for hanging. (On a star, for example, insert thread near one of the star points.)

Leave about 6 to 8 inches of thread evenly distributed on each side of the cookie. Extra thread can be trimmed away readily, but too little for easy tying may result in a broken cookie.

If raw dough tears, simply smooth out the cookie surface lightly with a fingertip.

Now apply decorations that should be baked on: whole or slivered almonds, colored sugars, dried or candied fruits and, of course, before-baking glazes.

Leave some shapes free of decoration to be decorated with frosting later.

After baking, threaded cookies are cooled on racks and stored according to the nature of the dough. They may be packaged and frozen, if prepared ahead.

NOTE: Prepare intricately cut or very small cookies for hanging by laying on cookie sheet and punching a hole in each with the blunt end of a toothpick but leave unthreaded. Decorate, if desired, then bake. While still warm and before removal from sheet, insert end of pick in hole again to reopen, if necessary. Thread after cooling on rack and before frosting.

Frosted cookies taste best if frosting is added just a day or two in advance of serving.

Easy to do and surprisingly effective when hung on a tree are simple shapes such as a star, deeply cut scallop or diamond

TO STRING COOKIES

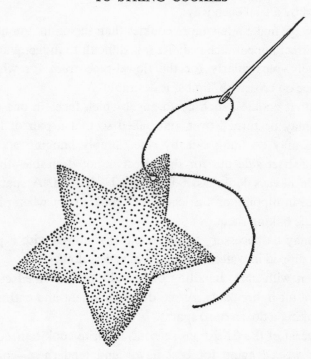

Before baking, run a 6"–8" piece of linen thread through cookies. If thread pulls too large a hole in dough, smooth and flatten with finger. For small, rich cookies that are likely to tear or pull out of shape with thread, punch holes in dough before baking with blunt end of toothpick. Be sure holes are large enough to accommodate needle and thread after baking. While cookies are hot and still on baking sheet, repunch holes with toothpick before removing to rack to cool.

outlined with white or tinted powdered sugar frosting forced through a decorating tube. Let frosting harden by exposure to air before attempting to hang cookies.

When ready to trim the cookie tree, knot the threads next to the cookie so that both ends may be pulled up close together. Form a hanging loop with the baked-in or added thread or tie it to a colored ribbon for attaching to the tree. Sometimes one effect is desirable, sometimes the other. Be guided by a trial each way.

Always make a few more cookies than the minimum needed for perfect appearance because it is difficult to judge quantities precisely—particularly for the dowel-type trees for which a balance on crosswise "limbs" is desirable.

Cutout cookies, such as an angel which faces in one direction, may be turned over and baked so that a pair of facing angels may be hung side by side. Simply hanging a cookie baking-sheet side out for this effect is not desirable—the underside always looks as if it should be hidden. A spatula is helpful in flipping an intricately cut cookie over when placing it on the baking sheet.

It may be necessary to brush the raw dough with a pastry brush dipped in water to free it from excess flour.

Even with care, handling of baked and decorated cookies may result in breakage. Avoid disappointment and extra work by making a dozen or so spares.

Several of the Christmas season's favorite cookies need four to six weeks' aging for best flavor and tenderness—consider early November as starting time on cookie making.

If you've a freezer, even the delicate butter cookies can be made one month ahead to be brought out proudly at the holidays with every assurance of goodness.

Many an old favorite with good keeping qualities such as

rolled ginger cookies (see Hildur's Gingersnaps and Molasses Dolls and Molasses Drops, quantity) has been made in November and eaten in January with as much relish as if baked the day before.

Included here are most old favorites of the season and a few tinseled surprises. Merry Christmas!

In this chapter are recipes for these Good Cookies:

PLAIN FANCY

BALL

Cardamom Balls

Christmas Cane Cookies

Pfeffernuesse II

Pfeffernuesse I

BARS

Butterscotch Shortbread

Chocolate Chip Shortbread

Chocolate Shortbread

LAYERED BARS

Cherry Cheese Dreams

DROP

Almond Sugar Cookies

Cherry Mounds

Butter Wafers

Fruit Drops

Condensed Milk Coconut

Fruit Lace Cookies

Drops

Holiday Macaroons

Macaroon Kisses

Ragged Robins

Peppermint Crunch

FILLED

Fruit-filled Tricornes

PLAIN   FANCY

ICEBOX

Marian's Pfeffernuesse   *Ribbon Cookies*

NO-BAKE

Bourbon Balls
Candied Fruit Drops

PRESSED

Chocolate Spritz I
Quick-mix Spritz
Sugar Plum Cookies

ROLLED

Buttermilk Sugar Cookies   *Fattigmand*
Cinnamon Crisps   *Katie's Springerle*
                                    Lebkuchen

Other recipes that could be included in this category are the following (to locate, see index):

BALL
  Frosted Snowballs
  Scandinavian Tea Cookies
DROP
  Anise Drops
  Gumdrop Jewels
PRESSED
  Wreath Cookies

ROLLED
  Molasses Dolls (*Gingerbread Men*)
  Nurembergers (*Honey Spice Daisies*)
SPECIALTY
  Gingerbread Houses
  Puffed Cereal House
  Sandbakelser

BALL COOKIES

Cardamom Balls [PLAIN]

Unforgettable flavor

½ cup shortening	½ teaspoon baking soda
½ cup sugar	1 teaspoon cinnamon
1 tablespoon molasses	¼ teaspoon ginger
½ teaspoon vanilla	¼ teaspoon cloves
1 egg	¼ teaspoon nutmeg
1¾ cups sifted all-purpose flour	¼ teaspoon allspice
½ teaspoon salt	6 cardamom seeds, hulled and ground

Cream shortening and sugar. Add molasses, vanilla and egg. Beat well. Sift together flour, salt, soda and spices. Stir crushed cardamom seeds into flour mixture. Add to shortening mixture, blending well. Form small balls. Bake on greased sheet at 375 degrees about 10 minutes. Avoid overbrowning or cookies will be hard. *4½ dozen*

Christmas Cane Cookies [FANCY]

Peppermint-sugar-glazed

½ cup butter
½ cup shortening
1 cup sifted powdered
    sugar
1 egg
1½ teaspoons almond
    extract
1 teaspoon vanilla

2½ cups sifted all-purpose
    flour
1 teaspoon salt
½ teaspoon red food
    coloring
½ cup crushed peppermint
    candy
½ cup granulated sugar

Blend butter and shortening together until smooth. Add powdered sugar, egg and flavorings. Gradually stir in sifted salt and flour. Divide dough in half. Add food coloring to one portion, blending until coloring is evenly mixed through dough. Roll 1 teaspoon of light dough and 1 teaspoon of pink dough into strips about 4 inches long. Place strips side by side, pressing lightly together. Twist like a rope. Place on ungreased cookie sheet, curving top like a cane handle. Bake at 375 degrees 10 minutes or until lightly browned. Remove to cooling rack. Combine crushed peppermint candy and granulated sugar. Sprinkle over warm cookies. *4 dozen*

Pfeffernuesse I [FANCY]

German favorite—well worth the effort

2 tablespoons butter
1¼ cups sifted powdered
    sugar
3 egg yolks
1 teaspoon grated lemon
    rind
½ pound candied citron
2 teaspoons crushed
    cardamom seed
½ teaspoon anise seed

2 cups sifted all-purpose
    flour
½ teaspoon baking soda
½ teaspoon salt
2 teaspoons cinnamon
½ teaspoon ground cloves
½ teaspoon nutmeg
⅛ teaspoon black pepper
3 egg whites

Glaze:

1½ cups sifted powdered
    sugar
3 tablespoons milk

Cream butter. Add sifted powdered sugar, then well-beaten egg yolks and lemon rind. Chop citron fine. Stir citron, crushed cardamom seed and anise seed into dry ingredients which have been sifted together three times. Add flour mixture to creamed ingredients. Beat egg whites stiff and fold into batter. Chill 1 hour. Form small balls and place on waxed paper. Let stand overnight. Brush cookies all over top and sides with glaze. Place balls on greased cookie sheet. Bake at 375 degrees 15 minutes. *4 dozen*

Pfeffernuesse II [PLAIN]

Excellent flavor in this version of the famous German cookie

½ cup corn syrup
½ cup molasses
¼ cup butter
½ cup less 2 tablespoons
brown sugar
1 tablespoon lemon juice
1 teaspoon grated lemon
rind

About 3 cups sifted all-
purpose flour
¼ teaspoon baking soda
½ teaspoon allspice
½ teaspoon cinnamon
⅛ teaspoon ground cloves
⅛ teaspoon white pepper
1 egg white

Warm corn syrup, molasses, butter, brown sugar, lemon juice and rind over low heat until sugar and butter melt. Remove from heat. Sift together dry ingredients and add, using a bit more flour if necessary to make an easily handled dough. (Too much flour will make cookies tough, so add sparingly, if at all.) Roll in ½-inch balls. Brush with slightly beaten egg white for glaze. Bake at 325 degrees 25 minutes or until golden brown. Cool. Roll in powdered sugar, if desired. Store in tightly closed container (a screw-top fruit jar is excellent) for at least a month before serving. Reroll in powdered sugar for a heavier coating at serving time. *5 to 6 dozen*

BAR COOKIES

Butterscotch Shortbread [PLAIN]

The familiar Scotch favorite enriched with brown sugar and nuts

½ cup butter
½ cup brown sugar, firmly packed
1 egg
1 teaspoon vanilla

2 cups sifted all-purpose flour
1 cup coarsely broken nut meats

Cream butter and sugar well. Blend in egg and vanilla. Add flour and nuts. Press in 8-inch-square pan. Mark in squares, pricking each with fork. Bake at 325 degrees 20 to 25 minutes. Cut into squares while warm. *2 dozen*

Chocolate Shortbread [PLAIN]

Sinfully rich—shatteringly crisp version of these Scotch cookies

2 squares or ounces unsweetened chocolate
1 cup butter
½ cup sifted powdered sugar

2 cups sifted all-purpose flour
¼ teaspoon salt
1 teaspoon vanilla

Melt chocolate, then cool. Cream butter well. Add powdered sugar, then sifted dry ingredients and cooled chocolate. Stir in vanilla. Press into 9-inch-square pan. Mark in squares, pricking each with fork. Bake at 325 degrees about 20 minutes. *3 dozen*

Chocolate Chip Shortbread [FANCY]

Gaily polka-dotted with chocolate bits

½ cup butter or margarine	½ teaspoon baking powder
1 cup sugar, white or brown	2 tablespoons cold water
2 eggs	½ teaspoon vanilla
1½ cups sifted all-purpose flour	1 6-ounce package semi-sweet chocolate bits

Cream butter and sugar. Beat in eggs. Sift together flour and baking powder and add alternately with water and vanilla. Stir in chocolate bits. Press into 9 × 13-inch pan. Mark into squares, pricking each with fork. Bake at 350 degrees 20 minutes. Cut into squares while warm. *3½ dozen*

LAYERED BAR COOKIES

Cherry Cheese Dreams [FANCY]

Pretty to look at, too

1¾ cups sifted all-purpose flour	½ cup brown sugar, firmly packed
1 teaspoon baking powder	½ cup butter or margarine
1 teaspoon cinnamon	1 cup grated sharp cheddar cheese

Sift together dry ingredients. Cut in butter and cheese until mixture is in fine crumbs. Press half the mixture firmly into an 8-inch-square pan. Spread with cooled filling.

Filling:

1 cup pitted tart cherries
1 cup brown sugar

Combine and boil till thick. Cool. Pour over crust. Cover with remaining cheese mixture. Bake at 350 degrees 30 to 35 minutes. Cool. Cut in squares. *2 dozen*

DROP COOKIES

Almond Sugar Cookies [PLAIN]

Delicately flavored

¾ cup butter
¾ cup sugar
1 egg, unbeaten
1 teaspoon vanilla
¼ teaspoon salt

⅔ cup blanched, finely
chopped almonds
1½ cups sifted all-purpose
flour

Cream butter and sugar well. Add egg, vanilla and salt, beating thoroughly. Blend in flour and almonds. Drop on lightly greased cookie sheet. Bake at 350 degrees 12 to 15 minutes. *4 dozen*

Butter Wafers [PLAIN]

Delightful with eggnog

¼ cup butter
¼ cup sugar
1 egg
½ cup sifted all-purpose
flour

¼ teaspoon salt
½ teaspoon vanilla
¼ teaspoon nutmeg

Cream butter. Add sugar and cream well. Add egg, then flour, salt, vanilla and nutmeg. Drop by small spoonfuls onto ungreased cookie sheet. Bake at 325 degrees about 12 minutes, until set and very lightly browned on edge. *4 dozen*

Cherry Mounds [FANCY]

Crisply coated with cereal

⅓ cup butter or margarine	1 teaspoon baking powder
½ cup sugar	1 cup chopped nuts
1 egg	1 cup crushed cereal flakes
1 teaspoon vanilla	(cornflakes, wheat flakes,
1½ tablespoons milk	etc.)
1 cup sifted all-purpose	24 maraschino cherries,
flour	halved
¼ teaspoon salt	

Cream butter and sugar. Add egg, vanilla and milk. Sift together dry ingredients and add. Stir in nuts. Spread crushed cereal flakes in shallow pan. Drop cookie dough by spoonfuls into cereal flakes. Coat well with crumbs. Place on baking sheet and top each cookie with half a cherry. Bake at 400 degrees about 10 minutes. *4 dozen*

Condensed Milk Coconut Drops [PLAIN]

Moist, chewy and very pretty

1 can (1⅓ cups) sweetened	½ cup chopped nuts
condensed milk	2 cups grated coconut
4 cups dry cereal flakes	
(cornflakes, wheat flakes,	
etc.)	

Pour condensed milk over combined cereal flakes, coconut and nuts. Stir to moisten well. Drop by spoonfuls onto well-greased baking sheet. Bake at 350 degrees 10 to 12 minutes. Remove quickly from cookie sheet. *5 dozen*

Fruit Drops [FANCY]

Rich as tiny fruitcakes

½ cup butter or margarine
1½ cups brown sugar
3 eggs, separated
2½ cups sifted flour
½ teaspoon baking soda
½ teaspoon baking powder
½ teaspoon salt
1 teaspoon cinnamon
1 teaspoon allspice
½ teaspoon nutmeg

½ cup sour cream
1 teaspoon brandy or
vanilla flavoring
1½ cups white seedless
raisins
1½ cups currants
1 pound mixed candied
fruits
1½ cups broken nut meats

Cream butter. Add sugar gradually, creaming well. Beat in egg yolks. Sift together dry ingredients and add alternately with sour cream. Add flavoring. Stir in fruits and nuts. Fold in stiffly beaten egg whites. Drop on greased cookie sheet. Bake at 325 degrees 20 to 25 minutes. *8 dozen*

Fruit Lace Cookies [FANCY]

Buffet specialty

1 cup diced candied fruits
¼ cup currants
¼ cup chopped, blanched
almonds or filberts
½ cup sifted all-purpose
flour

¼ cup butter
¼ cup sugar
1 tablespoon honey
1 teaspoon orange juice

Dredge fruits and nuts with the ½ cup flour. Melt butter and sugar. Add honey and orange juice, then stir in floured fruit and nut mixture, blending well. Drop on ungreased cookie sheet, spreading cookies well apart. Bake at 350 degrees 8 minutes. Let cool a minute, then cool on rack after lifting from sheet. Store loosely covered. *4 dozen*

Holiday Macaroons [FANCY]

Candied-fruit pretty

4 egg whites
1¼ cups sugar
¼ teaspoon salt
1 teaspoon vanilla

2½ cups cornflakes
½ cup finely cut candied fruit

Beat egg whites stiff. Beat in sugar gradually. Add salt and vanilla. Fold in cornflakes and candied fruit. Drop on lightly greased baking sheet. Bake at 325 degrees about 15 minutes. *3 dozen*

Macaroon Kisses [PLAIN]

Meringue-like with both nuts and coconut

5 egg whites
2 cups sugar
¼ cup sifted all-purpose flour

1 cup finely chopped nuts
1 cup grated coconut
1 teaspoon vanilla
¼ teaspoon salt

Beat egg whites until stiff. Beat in sugar gradually. Be sure sugar is thoroughly dissolved. Beat mixture until very stiff. Fold in sifted flour, nuts and coconut. Add vanilla and salt. Drop on lightly greased baking sheet. Bake at 325 degrees 12 to 15 minutes. Cool on rack. To keep crisp, store in cool, dry place in loosely covered container. *4 dozen*

[3] On rack in foreground *Mocha Nut Bars, Chocolate Nut Drops.* At right are *Coconut Fruit Cookies, Brownies I,* and *Rocky Road Bars.*

Color plate courtesy of General Foods Kitchens

[4] At either end of silver tray festive *Punch Bowl Cookies* are decorated with colored coconut (see Decorations section). In tray center are *Baked Candy Cookies* shaped in crescents and rolled in powdered sugar, just one of many possible variations.

⸝ Peppermint Crunch [PLAIN]

Holiday treat for children

¾ cup butter	½ teaspoon salt
1 cup sugar	3 cups flour
1 egg	¾ cup crushed peppermint
¼ cup milk	candy
2 teaspoons baking powder	

Cream shortening and sugar thoroughly. Add egg, beating well. Add milk. Sift together dry ingredients and add. Stir in candy. Drop on greased baking sheet. Bake at 375 degrees 10 to 12 minutes. *5 dozen*

⸝ Ragged Robins [FANCY]

Satisfying buffet dessert

2 egg whites	½ cup glazed cherries,
¼ teaspoon vanilla	quartered
⅛ teaspoon salt	1 cup walnut meats
½ pound dates, pitted and	1¾ cups cornflakes
chopped	½ cup white sugar

Beat egg whites until stiff. Add vanilla and salt. Combine remaining ingredients and add to egg-white mixture. Drop from spoon on greased baking sheet. Bake at 325 degrees for 15 minutes or until lightly brown. *3 dozen*

FILLED COOKIES

Fruit-filled Tricornes [FANCY]
Culinary magic

Dough:

½ cup shortening
1 cup sugar
2 eggs
2 tablespoons rich milk
1 teaspoon vanilla

2½ cups sifted all-purpose
  flour
½ teaspoon salt
½ teaspoon baking powder

Stir shortening until soft, blend in sugar. Beat in eggs until batter is smooth. Stir in milk and vanilla. Sift together dry ingredients and add to mixture, blending thoroughly. Chill dough 1 hour. Roll a small portion thin on lightly floured board. Cut into 2- or 3-inch rounds. Place 1 rounded teaspoon of thick Fruit Filling on top of each. Turn up edges to form a triangular cookie, leaving filling partially exposed. Bake at 400 degrees about 10 minutes, or until golden brown. *4 dozen*

FRUIT FILLINGS

Apricot Filling:

1 cup dried apricots
Water to cover
1 cup brown sugar

Boil apricots in water to cover 10 minutes. Drain and reserve liquid. Chop apricots. Stir brown sugar into apricots and add a tablespoon or so of reserved liquid if mixture seems dry. Cook and stir over low heat until sugar is dissolved and pasty in consistency. Watch carefully to prevent scorching. Cool.

Fig Filling:

1½ cups dried figs, chopped
⅓ cup sugar

¾ cup water
1 tablespoon lemon juice

Combine figs, sugar and water. Cook and stir until thick. Remove from heat. Add lemon juice. Cool.

Raisin Filling:

1½ cups ground raisins
⅔ cup sugar
2 tablespoons flour
¼ cup orange juice

¼ cup water
2 teaspoons grated orange rind

Combine raisins, sugar, flour, orange juice and water. Cook and stir until thick. Remove from heat. Add grated orange rind. Cool.

ICEBOX COOKIES

Marian's Pfeffernuesse [PLAIN]

No eggs in this version of the German holiday favorite

30 cardamom seeds
2 tablespoons anise seed
1½ cups butter or
   margarine
½ cup brown sugar, firmly
   packed

3 cups maple-flavored
   syrup
About 11 cups sifted flour
½ teaspoon salt
½ teaspoon baking soda
3 tablespoons cinnamon

Remove hulls from cardamom seeds. Place cardamom and anise seeds in preheated oven at 200 degrees for 10 minutes, then turn heat off and leave for 10 minutes longer. Remove from oven and put through fine knife of grinder or pound to crush fine.

Cream butter and brown sugar together with electric mixer,

blending well. Gradually add syrup with mixer on low speed, beating until batter is smooth. Sift together flour, salt, soda and cinnamon, stir in ground cardamom and anise. Stir flour mixture into butter mixture by hand in about four portions. Turn onto lightly floured board and knead well. If dough is too soft, additional flour may be kneaded in but avoid making dough hard with too much. Form into rolls and wrap well with two layers of waxed paper or one layer of heavy-duty aluminum foil. Store covered in refrigerator for at least 1 week. Slice thin. Bake on greased sheets at 325 degrees 25 to 30 minutes or until lightly browned. Glaze while warm by brushing with thin mixture of powdered sugar and water, if desired. *About 200*

Ribbon Cookies [FANCY]

Tricolored doughs

1 cup butter or margarine
1¼ cups sugar
1 egg
1 teaspoon vanilla
2½ cups sifted all-purpose flour
1¼ teaspoons baking powder

¼ teaspoon salt
1 ounce or square unsweetened chocolate, melted
¼ cup finely chopped nuts
2 tablespoons finely chopped candied cherries

Gradually add sugar to softened butter or margarine. Blend in egg and vanilla to a smooth batter. Sift flour, baking powder and salt. Add to mixture. Divide dough into three parts. Add melted chocolate and nuts to one portion; add cherries to another portion and leave one portion plain. Line a bread pan with aluminum foil, being sure to smooth corners. Pack in plain dough to a smooth layer. Cover with an even layer of chocolate-nut dough. Top with cherry dough. Cover with foil. Chill overnight. Lift dough from pan with foil. Slice thin and then cut each slice in half. Bake on lightly greased cookie sheet at 375 degrees 10 to 12 minutes. *3 dozen*

NO-BAKE COOKIES

Bourbon Balls [FANCY]

Excellent flavored with rum or brandy in place of bourbon

1 cup semi-sweet chocolate bits	2½ cups crushed vanilla wafers
3 tablespoons light corn syrup	½ cup powdered sugar
½ cup bourbon or light cream	1 cup chopped nuts

Melt chocolate bits over hot water. Add corn syrup and bourbon or substitute. Combine vanilla wafer crumbs, powdered sugar and nuts. Add chocolate mixture. (If cream is used, add ½ teaspoon vanilla.) Let stand 30 minutes. Shape in 1-inch balls. Roll in granulated or powdered sugar. Let ripen in covered container at least three days. *About 4 dozen*

Candied Fruit Drops [FANCY]

Keep these ready to serve in a freezer

1 cup brown sugar	1 teaspoon grated orange rind
¾ cup top milk	
2 tablespoons corn syrup	½ cup mixed candied fruits, finely chopped
¼ teaspoon salt	
2 tablespoons margarine	¾ cup quick rolled oats

Combine sugar, milk, corn syrup and salt. Bring to boil and cook to soft-ball stage (236 degrees). Remove from heat.

Stir in margarine and orange rind. Cool 5 minutes. Stir in candied fruits and rolled oats, blending thoroughly. Drop in small mounds on waxed paper. When cool, wrap individually in Saran Wrap. Store in refrigerator for short storage and in freezer for long storage. *2½ to 3 dozen*

PRESSED COOKIES

Chocolate Spritz I [PLAIN]

Widely renowned

1 cup butter	1½ teaspoons vanilla
⅔ cup sugar	½ teaspoon baking powder
3 egg yolks	2½ cups sifted all-purpose
2 ounces or squares	flour
unsweetened chocolate,	
melted	

Cream butter, add sugar and slightly beaten egg yolks. Stir in melted, cooled chocolate and vanilla. Sift together dry ingredients and add. Form cookies with press on ungreased cookie sheet. Bake at 375 degrees 8 to 10 minutes. *5 dozen*

NOTE: This dough is a fine basic Spritz, if chocolate is eliminated. Add ½ teaspoon almond extract to light dough in place of ½ teaspoon vanilla. Form and bake as directed.

Quick-mix Spritz [PLAIN]

Swedish treat made in jiffy time

2¼ cups sifted all-purpose flour	1 cup shortening
¾ cup sugar	1 egg
¼ teaspoon baking powder	Water, if needed
½ teaspoon salt	1 teaspoon vanilla
	½ teaspoon almond extract

Sift dry ingredients into mixing bowl. Cut in shortening with pastry blender as for pie crust. Break egg into a measuring cup. If egg does not measure ¼ cup, add water to ¼-cup level. Add egg and flavorings to shortening mixture, blending well. Put through cookie press on ungreased baking sheet. Bake at 375 degrees 10 to 12 minutes. *4½ dozen*

Sugar Plum Cookies [PLAIN]

Sugared and spiced

1 cup butter	2¼ cups sifted all-purpose flour
1 3-ounce package cream cheese	½ teaspoon salt
1 cup sugar	¼ teaspoon baking powder
1 egg yolk	½ cup sugar, additional
1¼ teaspoons vanilla	2 teaspoons cinnamon

Blend butter and room-temperature cream cheese until well mixed. Cream in 1 cup sugar gradually. Add egg yolk and vanilla. Sift together dry ingredients and add in three or four parts, blending thoroughly after each addition. Form cookies with press on ungreased cookie sheet. Combine ½ cup sugar and cinnamon, stirring well. Place in clean salt shaker and sprinkle sugar-spice mixture over unbaked cookies. Bake at 350 degrees 12 to 15 minutes or until lightly browned. *5½ dozen*

ROLLED COOKIES

Buttermilk Sugar Cookies [PLAIN]

None better

1 cup shortening	¼ cup buttermilk
1 cup sugar	¼ teaspoon baking powder
1 egg	1 teaspoon salt
1 teaspoon vanilla	About 3 cups sifted
½ teaspoon baking soda	all-purpose flour

Cream shortening, blend in sugar. Add slightly beaten egg and vanilla. Dissolve soda in buttermilk, then add to creamed mixture. Sift together 2 cups flour, salt and baking powder. Add to mixture. Add enough more flour so that dough will roll easily on lightly floured board. Dough may be chilled 1 hour or longer, if desired, to make handling easier with less flour. (Too much flour will make cookies tough.) Roll thin, cut with floured cutters into desired shapes. Place on ungreased cookie sheet. Bake at 400 degrees 8 to 10 minutes. Do not overbrown. *6 dozen*

Cinnamon Crisps [PLAIN]

Sour-cream-enriched

½ cup butter	½ teaspoon salt
½ cup sugar	2 cups sifted all-purpose
1 egg	flour
1 teaspoon vanilla	½ cup sour cream
¼ teaspoon baking soda	2 teaspoons cinnamon
½ teaspoon baking powder	½ cup sugar, additional

Cream butter. Add sugar. Beat in egg and vanilla thoroughly. Sift together soda, baking powder, salt and flour and add to mixture alternately with sour cream. Chill 1 hour. Roll on lightly floured board and cut as desired. Place on cookie sheet. Combine ½ cup sugar and cinnamon and sprinkle over cookies. Bake on ungreased cookie sheet 8 to 10 minutes at 400 degrees. *4 dozen*

Fattigmand [FANCY]

A foreign delicacy from Norway

3 eggs	⅛ teaspoon crushed cardamom seed
3 tablespoons sugar	
⅛ teaspoon grated lemon rind	3 tablespoons heavy cream
	About 1½ cups sifted all-purpose flour
1/16 teaspoon cinnamon	

Beat eggs until smoothly thickened and light in color. Beat in gradually sugar, spices and lemon rind. Add cream. Gradually stir in flour until dough is just stiff enough to handle. Chill 4 hours. Roll out one third of dough at a time very thin on lightly floured board. Use fluted pastry wheel or knife to cut diamond-shaped pieces about 3 inches long. Cut a 1-inch gash in one end of the diamond-shaped dough and slip point through. Drop into 375-degree deep fat. Cook until delicately browned, turning once, about 30 seconds on a side. Drain on kitchen paper towels. Sift powdered sugar over cookies when ready to serve. *About 4 dozen*

Katie's Springerle [FANCY]

Christmas treat from Germany

12 eggs
3 pounds powdered sugar, sifted
10 cups flour
¾ cup soft butter
2 teaspoons anise oil

Juice and grated rind of 1 lemon
2 teaspoons ammonium carbonate, ground fine (secured from large drugstores)

Beat eggs very thoroughly. Beat in powdered sugar gradually. When all has been added, continue to beat batter about 15 to 20 minutes. Then mix in all other ingredients, adding flour about 2 cups at a time. When all blended, beat batter another 15 minutes or so. Chill dough several hours for easier handling. Roll a small portion at a time on lightly floured board to ¼-inch thickness. Flour a carved springerle pin or board generously, then roll or press design into dough. Cut cookies apart. Lay on well-greased cookie sheets. Sheets may be sprinkled lightly with whole anise seed before unbaked cookies are placed on them, if desired. Leave cookies uncovered at room temperature overnight. Bake 15 to 20 minutes at 325 degrees. Cool. Store in tightly closed container several weeks to mellow. *About 200 small cookies*

Lebkuchen [FANCY]

A holiday favorite imported from Germany

¾ cup honey
1 cup brown sugar
2 tablespoons water
¼ cup shortening
2 eggs
¼ teaspoon baking soda
¼ teaspoon salt

3¼ cups sifted all-purpose flour
2 teaspoons cinnamon
1 teaspoon cardamom
¼ teaspoon nutmeg
¼ cup citron, chopped fine (optional)

Combine honey, brown sugar and water and boil 5 minutes. Add shortening, stir to blend. When slightly cooled, add well-beaten eggs, then sift together dry ingredients and add. Stir in citron. Pat dough into compact ball in casserole and chill, covered, in refrigerator at least 3 days. Roll dough on lightly floured board, a fourth at a time, and cut into bars. Place on greased baking sheet. Bake at 325 degrees 15 to 20 minutes. While still warm, spread with Lebkuchen Glaze. *About 4 dozen*

Lebkuchen Glaze:
½ cup sifted powdered sugar
2 tablespoons boiling water
½ teaspoon vanilla

Combine and spread over warm bars.

Cookies with a Foreign Accent

Neighborly recipe exchange no longer means just with the charming lady down the block—it may well be with a friend or pen pal across an ocean and a continent or so. A taste for good cookies is international.

Some of the foreign cookies have become so much a part of American tradition, one forgets that their original home is far away. Who thinks of gingersnaps as Swedish or rolled honey bars as German?

Truly treasures are individual cookies distinctive enough to have retained not only their original character but their native names: Springerle, Pfeffernuesse, Spritz, Sandbakelser and Shortbread are some of these.

Perhaps flavor is the significant difference between cookies native to this country and those of foreign origin. Mexican Rolled Cookies, for example, are made from a rich dough of proportions not very different from many old favorites. What makes them peculiarly individual is the inclusion of cinnamon both inside the dough mixture and in the spicy sugar topping sprinkled over the baked cookie before cooling.

Caraway, anise and poppy seeds—characteristic of Middle European cookery—give distinctive flavor to the cookies in which they are used. The goodness of these is found in many forms of baked and cooked dishes from casseroles to cakes, providing persons familiar with the taste a nostalgic memory and for newcomers a pleasurable surprise.

Pastry-like doughs that can be rolled easily are a perfect foil for the sweet, fruity filling in the Crescents that can be made with cottage cheese, cream cheese or sour cream. These retain the aura of their Austrian homeland where they are served often with coffee.

Another happy choice for accompanying a cup of coffee or tea is the Polish Tea Thin, so versatile in goodness that it is served in three ways: Plain, jam-filled and frosted. Make them small in any case, and be sure baking is done just to a point of delicate creaminess in color like old ivory.

Danish Wreaths, fashioned from a rope of dough, have a delightful party look as well as distinctive flavor. Choose from three versions, one rich in golden egg yolks, one textured with rolled oats and another flavored delicately with brandy and nutmeg.

Beloved for an unusual, light crispness of texture and the sleek nut meat centering each are Chinese Almond Cookies. For busy-day baking, there's a sliced, icebox version of this imported delicacy that uses finely chopped almonds in the dough.

Occasionally one finds it necessary to provide oneself with special tools to make the foreign cookies. Special irons for Rosettes, a cookie press, a collection of fluted tart pans and a group of tiny imported Swedish cookie cutters belong in the kitchen of a true cookie lover. Skillfully carved springerle boards and rolling pins made by European artisans are available to give these cookies their picturesque motifs.

On the other hand, many of the foreign cookies require no unusual equipment or ingredients. And recipes have been translated from the foreign weights and measures into readily understood American measurements so that no difficulty will be encountered on that score.

Be not leery of a recipe that calls for ammonium carbonate. It is a standard leavening agent in many foreign countries and, when used in quantities specified and according to directions, assures a light cookie of great delicacy. Large drugstores can supply it in most areas.

On to traveling via the kitchen range!

In this chapter are recipes for these Good Cookies:

PLAIN   FANCY

BALLS

Anna's Snaps—Swedish   *Eggnog Wreaths—Danish*
Butter Nut Balls and   *Scandinavian Tea Cookies*
   Variations—European
Chinese Almond Cookies
Danish Wreaths I
Danish Wreaths II

BARS

Caraway Sponge Bars
   —Italian

DROP

Anise Drops—German
Poppy Seed Wafers
   —Austrian

ICEBOX

Chinese Almond Slices
Danish Crisps

PRESSED

Spritz—Swedish   *Crown Cookies—French*

ROLLED

Butter Rings—Scandinavian

Hildur's Gingersnaps
  —Swedish

Honey Spice Daisies
    (Nurembergers)
  —German

Mexican Rolled Cookies

Polish Tea Thins

Shortbread—Scotch

Crescents—Cottage Cheese
  —Austrian

Crescents—Cream Cheese
  —French

Crescents—Sour Cream
  —Mid-European

Polish Tea Thins—Filled

Polish Tea Thins—Frosted

SPECIALTY

Almond-filled Tarts
  —Scandinavian

Almond Pastry Tarts
  —Scandinavian

Rosettes—Swedish

Sandbakelser
  —Scandinavian

Other recipes that could be included in this category are the following (to locate, see index):

BALL
  Pfeffernuesse I
  Pfeffernuesse II
PRESSED
  Danish Wreaths
ROLLED
  Brazilian Treats
  Fattigmand
  Lebkuchen
  Rich Rolled Cookies
  Springerle

BALL COOKIES

Anna's Snaps [PLAIN]

Deliciously crisp and sugar-coated Swedish treats

¾ cup butter
1 cup brown sugar, firmly
  packed
1 egg
3 tablespoons molasses
2½ cups all-purpose flour,
  not sifted

2 teaspoons baking soda
¼ teaspoon salt
1 teaspoon cinnamon
½ teaspoon ginger
½ teaspoon cloves

Blend brown sugar into soft butter well. Stir in egg and molasses. Sift together dry ingredients and add gradually. Chill overnight. Form small balls and dip in granulated sugar. Place on greased sheet. Sprinkle 2 drops water on top of each. Bake at 350 degrees 10 to 12 minutes. *About 5 dozen*

Butter Nut Balls and Variations [PLAIN]

Rich, crisp—with three versions of this cookie popular throughout Europe

1 cup butter
½ cup sifted powdered
  sugar
1 teaspoon vanilla
⅛ teaspoon salt

2¼ cups sifted all-purpose
  flour
¾ cup chopped nuts (al-
  monds, Brazil nuts, filberts, pecans or walnuts)

Beat butter until soft. Add powdered sugar. Stir in vanilla and salt. Add flour gradually. Work in nuts thoroughly. Chill dough 1 hour. Form 1-inch balls. Bake on ungreased sheet at 400 degrees 10 to 12 minutes. Dough should be set but not brown. Roll while warm in sifted powdered sugar. Cool. Roll in powdered sugar again. *4 dozen*

VARIATIONS

Norwegian Cookies: Decorated with candied fruit. Shape dough in ½-inch balls. Garnish with a piece of candied fruit. Place on ungreased sheet. Bake at 350 degrees 10 minutes. *5½ to 6 dozen smaller cookies*

Almond Balls: Traditional Christmas favorite. Use only ½ teaspoon vanilla and add ½ teaspoon almond extract. Use ¾ cup blanched almonds, ground fine. Shape in balls or crescents. Bake at 375 degrees until set but not brown, about 10 minutes. *4 to 5 dozen*

Chinese Almond Cookies [PLAIN]

Dainty and delicate in flavor

⅓ cup butter	¼ teaspoon salt
⅓ cup shortening	1 tablespoon milk
½ cup sugar	½ teaspoon almond extract
1½ cups sifted all-purpose flour	2 egg whites
1½ teaspoons baking powder	Whole blanched almonds

Blend soft butter and shortening together well. Cream in sugar. Sift together dry ingredients and add alternately with milk and almond extract. Fold in stiffly beaten egg whites. Roll teaspoonfuls of dough in granulated sugar. Place balls on greased cookie sheet. Press a whole almond in center of each. Bake at 325 degrees about 12 to 15 minutes. *3½ to 4 dozen*

Danish Wreaths I [PLAIN]

Golden in color, rich in flavor

½ cup butter
½ cup sugar
2 hard-cooked egg yolks, sieved
2 raw egg yolks
4 tablespoons cream

1 teaspoon vanilla
¼ teaspoon almond extract
2 cups sifted all-purpose flour
Glazed fruit and nuts for garnish

Cream butter and sugar. Add sieved egg yolks. Stir raw egg yolks, cream and flavorings together. Add alternately with flour to butter mixture. Pinch off a ball of dough. Roll to a strip and shape into a wreath, crossing ends to form a knot. Decorate with chopped nuts or glazed fruits. If glazed cookies are desired, brush dough with slightly beaten white of egg. Bake on lightly greased sheet at 425 degrees 8 to 10 minutes. *3 dozen*

Danish Wreaths II [PLAIN]

Less rich than Wreaths I, with rolled oats for "nutty" flavor

¾ cup butter
½ cup sugar
1 teaspoon vanilla
¼ teaspoon almond flavoring
1¼ cups sifted all-purpose flour

¾ cup rolled oats
1 egg white
2 tablespoons sugar, additional
Candied fruit and nuts for garnish

Cream together soft butter and ½ cup sugar until smoothly blended. Beat in flavorings. Add flour in three additions, then work in rolled oats, using hands to knead the stiff batter. Chill 2 hours. Pinch off ball of dough and work with fingers until pliable. Roll to a strip and form a wreath, crossing ends for a knot. Prepare glaze of 1 egg white beaten until stiff, then gradually beat in 2 tablespoons sugar. Arrange wreath cookies on ungreased sheet. Brush with glaze. Decorate with nuts or candied fruits. Bake at 375 degrees 10 minutes or until lightly browned. *3 dozen*

Eggnog Wreaths [FANCY]

Quickly shaped but pretty and delicious Danish cookie

⅔ cup butter
⅓ cup sugar
2 tablespoons brandy or
  1 teaspoon brandy extract
  and 5 teaspoons water
¼ teaspoon salt

1¾ cups sifted all-purpose flour
2 tablespoons sugar, additional
1 teaspoon freshly grated nutmeg

Cream butter until soft. Blend in ⅓ cup sugar. Stir in brandy or substitute. Sift together salt and flour and add. Chill dough 30 minutes. Roll 1-inch ball of dough, then form into long strip. Make wreath of strip, crossing ends of dough rope-fashion. Combine 2 tablespoons sugar with grated nutmeg. Sprinkle over wreaths. Place on lightly greased cookie sheet. Bake at 400 degrees 8 to 10 minutes, until dough is set but not browned. *About 3 dozen*

Scandinavian Tea Cookies [FANCY]

Dainty nut-coated, red-centered tidbits

1 cup butter
½ cup brown sugar
2 egg yolks
1 teaspoon vanilla
2 cups sifted all-purpose flour

1 egg white
1 cup shaved almonds or finely chopped pecans, filberts or walnuts
Red jelly or candied cherries

Cream butter. Beat in sugar and slightly beaten egg yolks

and vanilla. Add flour. Form 1-inch balls. Dip in slightly beaten egg white and then in chopped or shaved nuts. Place on baking sheet 3 inches apart. Make depression in center of each. Bake at 350 degrees 10 minutes. Remove from oven. Press centers down again. Return to oven to finish baking, about 5 minutes longer. Remove to cooling rack. While still warm but not hot, fill centers with red jelly or half a candied red or green cherry. *4 dozen*

BAR COOKIES

Caraway Sponge Bars [PLAIN]

Light, delicate Italian favorite

3 eggs, separated
½ cup granulated sugar
1 teaspoon grated lemon rind

¾ cup sifted all-purpose flour
1 tablespoon fresh caraway seed (or anise or poppy seed)

Beat egg whites until stiff. Beat yolks until thick and lemon-colored. Gradually beat sugar and lemon rind into yolks. Fold in sifted flour and seeds. Fold in stiffly beaten egg whites. Pour into 9-inch-square pan lined with waxed paper. Bake at 375 degrees 15 to 20 minutes. Cool on rack. Cut into squares. *16 squares*

DROP COOKIES

Anise Drops [PLAIN]

Tops puff up like icing on this traditional German cookie

2 eggs
1 cup sugar
¼ teaspoon salt
1 teaspoon vanilla or grated
  lemon rind

2 cups sifted all-purpose
  flour
1½ tablespoons crushed
  anise seed

Beat eggs until thick and lemon-colored. Gradually add sugar, continuing to beat until very, very thick. Fold in flavoring. Fold in sifted flour gradually, then add anise seed. Drop onto lightly greased cookie sheets. Let stand until hard crusts form on top, about 12 hours. Bake at 350 degrees about 10 minutes. Tops puff up to resemble icing. Store in tightly covered container. *3 dozen*

Poppy Seed Wafers [PLAIN]

Glazed, sugar- and seed-topped goodies from Austria

1 cup butter or margarine
½ cup sifted powdered
  sugar
2½ cups sifted all-purpose
  flour

2 eggs, beaten
1 teaspoon grated lemon
  rind
3 tablespoons poppy seed

Cream butter well. Blend in sifted powdered sugar and flour. Reserve 3 tablespoons of beaten egg for glazing. Add remaining egg to butter mixture. Add lemon rind. Drop on ungreased baking sheet. Flatten with flat-bottomed glass dipped in sugar. Brush tops with 3 tablespoons beaten egg, then sprinkle with poppy seed. Bake at 350 degrees 12 to 15 minutes. *4 dozen*

ICEBOX COOKIES

Chinese Almond Slices [PLAIN]

Crispy with chopped almonds

1 cup sugar	¾ cup margarine
1¾ cups sifted all-purpose flour	½ teaspoon almond extract
	2 egg whites
½ teaspoon baking powder	1 cup chopped or ground
¼ teaspoon nutmeg	unblanched almonds

Sift together dry ingredients three times, the last time into mixing bowl. Cut in room-temperature margarine. Add almond extract and unbeaten egg whites, stirring until flour mixture is all dampened. Add nuts and blend well. Shape into rolls. Wrap in waxed paper or aluminum foil. Chill 4 hours. Slice thin. Bake on ungreased sheet at 375 degrees 8 to 10 minutes. *About 4 dozen*

Danish Crisps [PLAIN]

Dainty in both flavor and texture

⅔ cup shortening	½ teaspoon vanilla
¾ cup sugar	2 cups sifted all-purpose flour
1 egg	
2 teaspoons grated lemon or orange rind	½ teaspoon salt
	1 teaspoon baking powder

Cream shortening, gradually adding sugar. Stir in egg until well blended. Add grated rind and vanilla. Sift together dry ingredients and add in three parts, working in well. Form dough into two long rolls on waxed paper or aluminum foil.

Chill 4 hours. Slice, place on ungreased cookie sheet. Bake at 375 degrees 10 minutes or until lightly browned on edges. *About 5 dozen*

PRESSED COOKIES

Crown Cookies [FANCY]

Regally good French delicacy

½ cup butter	¼ teaspoon vanilla
¼ cup sugar	1¼ cups sifted all-purpose
1 egg	flour
½ teaspoon almond extract	Glazed fruits for garnish

Cream butter until soft, then stir in sugar gradually. Add egg and flavorings. Gradually add flour. Form cookies with press on ungreased sheet. Garnish with bits of candied fruits for jewel effect. Bake at 375 degrees 8 to 10 minutes. *2½ dozen*

Spritz [PLAIN]

An easy-to-handle recipe for this Swedish favorite

1½ cups butter	1 teaspoon baking powder
1 cup sugar	4 cups sifted all-purpose
1 egg	flour
1 teaspoon vanilla	Chopped nuts, candied
1 teaspoon almond extract	cherries or colored deco-
¼ teaspoon salt	rating sugars, if desired

Cream butter until very soft. Work in sugar, then egg and vanilla. Sift together dry ingredients and add gradually. Form cookies with press on ungreased cookie sheet, decorating as desired. Bake at 400 degrees about 8 to 10 minutes. *About 7½ dozen*

ROLLED COOKIES

Butter Rings [PLAIN]

The famous cinnamon-glazed Scandinavian favorite

5 tablespoons whipping cream

2 cups sifted all-purpose flour

1 cup butter

2 teaspoons cinnamon

½ cup sugar

Mix cream with flour. Pat dough out on floured board. Cut butter in bits to dot over surface of dough. Fold dough over in thirds so that butter is within the layers. Gently roll dough. Chill dough 30 minutes. Again fold and roll dough several times so that butter is worked evenly throughout. Be sure to keep dough cold. Roll out one third of dough at a time, chilling remainder. Cut into rings with floured doughnut cutter. Bake at 375 degrees 8 to 10 minutes. Combine sugar and cinnamon and dip hot cookies in spice mixtures. *3½ to 4 dozen*

Crescents—Cottage Cheese [FANCY]

Delightful treats in the tradition of Austrian pastry

1 cup butter

½ pint small-curd, dry cottage cheese

1 tablespoon sour cream

¼ teaspoon salt

2 cups flour

Milk or 1 slightly beaten egg white for glaze

1 cup jam or preserves (apricot, berry, peach or plum)

Cream room-temperature butter, then blend in dry cottage cheese which has been forced through fine sieve, and sour cream. Add sifted salt and flour. Chill dough 2 hours. Roll a portion of dough at a time, rolling thin on lightly floured board. Cut in 3-inch squares, then triangles. Place a bit of jam in center, then roll dough, beginning at wide end. Curve rolls into crescent shape and place on ungreased baking sheet. Brush tops of cookies with milk or egg white beaten with 2 tablespoons water for glaze. Bake at 400 degrees about 20 minutes. *About 2½ dozen*

Crescents—Cream Cheese [FANCY]

Jam-filled tiny French pastries

1 8-ounce package cream cheese	2 cups sifted all-purpose flour
1 cup butter	1 cup jam or preserves
¼ teaspoon salt	(peach, berry, apricot or plum)

Let cream cheese and butter soften to room temperature, then cream together well. Stir in sifted salt and flour. Chill dough 2 hours. Roll one third of dough at a time on lightly floured board. Cut in 3-inch squares, then triangles. Place jam in center of dough and roll up, beginning at wide end. Curve into crescent shape. Place on ungreased baking sheet. Bake at 400 degrees 20 minutes or until light gold color. *2 to 2½ dozen*

Crescents—Sour Cream [FANCY]

Richest and flakiest of all versions of this mid-European delicacy

2 Batches

3 cups sifted all-purpose flour	2 egg yolks, beaten
1 teaspoon salt	Milk or 1 beaten egg white for glaze
½ cup lard	1 cup jam or preserves (apricot, berry, plum or peach)
½ cup butter	
1 cup thick sour cream	

Sift flour and salt into mixing bowl. Cut in shortenings until well mixed but not greasy. Stir slightly beaten yolks and cream together and add to shortening mixture, pressing dough lightly with fingertips until smooth ball is formed. Divide dough into three flat balls and chill 30 minutes. Roll out one ball at a time on lightly floured board. Cut into 3-inch squares, then triangles. Place a little jam in center of each triangle and roll up, beginning at wide end. Curve into crescent shape. Place on ungreased cookie sheet. Brush tops with milk or 1 egg white beaten slightly with 2 tablespoons water. Dust lightly with colored sugars or nutmeg, if desired. Bake at 400 degrees about 20 minutes. *2 to 2½ dozen*

Hildur's Gingersnaps [PLAIN]

Delicately crisp and delicious Swedish cookies

1 cup heavy sour cream	½ teaspoon cloves
1 cup molasses or dark corn syrup or part of each	½ teaspoon baking soda
½ cup brown sugar	¼ teaspoon salt
1 teaspoon cinnamon	4 cups flour or enough to make soft dough
½ teaspoon ginger	

Stir together sour cream, molasses or corn syrup and brown

sugar. Sift together dry ingredients and add, blending well. Dough should be soft. Chill overnight. Roll dough on lightly floured board. Cut with floured cutters. Bake on greased baking sheet 8 to 10 minutes at 375 degrees. *5 to 6 dozen*

Honey Spice Daisies [PLAIN]

The same recipe as famous German Nurembergers

2½ cups sifted all-purpose flour
½ teaspoon baking soda
½ teaspoon cloves
1 teaspoon cinnamon
1 teaspoon allspice
¼ teaspoon ground cardamom
½ cup chopped nuts
½ cup chopped candied orange peel
1 cup strained honey
¾ cup brown sugar, firmly packed
1 egg
1 tablespoon lemon juice
1 teaspoon grated lemon rind
Blanched almonds for garnish
Candied lemon peel for garnish

Sift together flour and spices. Chop nuts and candied orange peel very fine. Heat combined honey and brown sugar just to boiling. Cool. Add slightly beaten egg, lemon juice and grated lemon rind. Then gradually stir in flour mixture, adding nuts and orange peel last. Chill dough overnight. Roll on lightly floured board, about ¼ inch thick. Cut into small round cookies, place on lightly greased baking sheet and decorate to resemble daisies by placing strips of almonds and candied lemon peel in petal formation, pressing into dough lightly. Bake at 350 degrees 8 to 10 minutes. Cool on rack. Store in closely covered container about a week before using. *4 dozen*

Mexican Rolled Cookies [PLAIN]

Crisp, rich, cinnamon-coated goodies

1 cup butter or margarine
2 cups sugar
¼ teaspoon baking powder
⅛ teaspoon salt
2 cups sifted all-purpose
flour

1 teaspoon cinnamon
⅓ cup sugar, additional
1 teaspoon cinnamon,
additional

Cream butter, then add 2 cups sugar gradually. Sift together flour, baking powder, salt and 1 teaspoon cinnamon. Add to creamed mixture in three parts, mixing well. Roll ¼ inch thick on lightly floured board. Cut with 2½-inch round floured cutter. Bake 10 to 12 minutes at 400 degrees. Mix ⅓ cup sugar and 1 teaspoon cinnamon. Sprinkle hot cookies with mixture. *About 4 dozen*

Polish Tea Thins [PLAIN]

Dainty and crisp with finely chopped nuts

1 cup butter
½ cup sugar
¼ teaspoon vanilla

2 cups sifted all-purpose
flour
¼ teaspoon salt
1 cup finely chopped nuts

Cream butter until soft, then blend in sugar, vanilla and sifted flour and salt mixture. Add nuts. Roll on lightly floured board as thin as may be easily handled. Cut in small rounds. Bake 8 to 10 minutes at 375 degrees. Do not overbrown. *4 dozen*

Polish Tea Thins—Filled [FANCY]

Delicious raspberry jam cookie "sandwiches"

1 recipe dough for Polish Tea Thins, baked according to recipe above
1 cup raspberry jam

Make small sandwich-style cookies by spreading one cooled cookie with raspberry jam, then topping with another. Dust top cookie with powdered sugar. *2 dozen*

Polish Tea Thins—Frosted [FANCY]

Chocolate frosting makes them even better

1 recipe dough for Polish Tea Thins, baked according to recipe above

½ recipe Chocolate Frosting (see index)

Top each cookie with thin coating of chocolate frosting and place on rack until frosting is set.

Shortbread [PLAIN]

Time-honored recipe from Scotland

1 pound (2 cups) fresh butter
½ pound (1 cup) sugar
1 pound (4 cups) flour

½ teaspoon salt
½ teaspoon vanilla
Blanched almond halves

Cream butter until almost white. Blend in sugar and beat vigorously. Stir in sifted salt and flour in four parts, working into dough thoroughly. Roll out dough or press into 9-inch-square pan, cutting into squares, oblongs or diamonds. Prick each piece with fork tines. Decorate each with almond half. Bake at 300 degrees 20 to 25 minutes. Dough should turn golden but not brown at all during baking. If baked in square pan, cut cookies again after baking and separate. *About 3 dozen*

SPECIALTY

Almond-filled Tarts [FANCY]

Delicate, crisp Scandinavian confection baked in fluted pans

½ cup butter
½ cup sifted powdered
    sugar
¼ teaspoon almond extract

2 egg yolks
1½ cups sifted all-purpose
    flour
Almond Filling

Cream butter and sugar together well. Add almond extract. Add slightly beaten egg yolks. Stir in flour gradually, working dough thoroughly after all flour is added. Chill dough 10 to 15 minutes. Coat fluted tart pans with dough evenly and thinly. Add 1 tablespoon of Almond Filling. Bake at 400 degrees about 15 minutes or until pastry is browned and filling set. Cool slightly before removing from pans. *2 dozen*

Almond Filling:
2 eggs, well beaten
1 cup sugar

1 cup finely ground
    blanched almonds

Blend to a heavy sauce. Cover and store in refrigerator until ready for use.

Almond Pastry Tarts [FANCY]

Famed Scandinavian sweet pastry

1 recipe pastry for Almond-filled Tarts

⅔ cup finely ground blanched almonds

Add almonds to pastry. Coat small fluted tins with chilled dough. Bake at 400 degrees 8 to 10 minutes or until lightly browned. Cool in pans. Serve plain, dusted with powdered sugar or filled with a bit of colorful jam or marmalade. These cookies may also serve as cups for whipping cream or ice cream. *2 dozen*

Rosettes [FANCY]

Beautiful Swedish fried delicacies

2 eggs
2 teaspoons sugar
1 cup milk

¼ teaspoon salt
1 cup flour
Deep fat for frying

Beat eggs very slightly, then beat in sugar until barely mixed. Add milk. Add sifted salt and flour. Beat until smooth as heavy cream. Heat deep fat to 375 degrees. Heat rosette iron in hot fat about 60 seconds. Dip hot iron into batter, making sure batter does not reach over the top of iron. Dip batter-coated iron into hot fat, deep enough to cover batter. Cook to golden brown, about 1½ to 2 minutes. Drain on kitchen paper toweling. Reheat iron in hot fat before dipping again into batter. Sprinkle rosettes with powdered sugar before serving. *About 3 dozen*

Sandbakelser [FANCY]

Scandinavian tarts to serve filled or not

1½ cups butter	½ teaspoon almond extract
⅞ cup sugar	4 cups sifted all-purpose
1 egg yolk	flour

Cream butter well. Gradually cream in sugar. Add egg yolk and vanilla and mix to blend well. Gradually stir in flour. Chill dough 30 minutes. Press a small ball of dough evenly and thinly over the inside of tiny fluted tart pans. Bake at 425 degrees until golden brown, about 10 minutes. (Chill unused portion of dough during baking.) Cool slightly and remove from pans. Serve plain, dusted with powdered sugar or filled with thickened, tart fruit juice. *About 4 dozen small tarts*

Cookie Spectaculars

There is nothing quite like the satisfaction of creating your own work of art, particularly if it is one you know will add a note of pleasure for the family, gathering at a celebration, or make the table gay for some special party.

In the recipes that follow, you will find cookies that vary widely in flavor, shape and purpose. All have been chosen because they have at least one spectacular feature—be it taste, form or unique combination of ingredients. All these spectacular cookies are the kind to put you in the ranks of those who come up with "something different."

While all earn the title of "spectacular" not all are time-consuming or difficult by any means. The Black and White Balls, Chocolate Cherry Balls, Crunchies and Butter Nut Wafers are no more complicated than the more familiar cookies of their particular types. It is the combinations of ingredients that make them outstanding.

Some, however, are frankly the kind that say, "This is an occasion," a flattering compliment to your guests regardless of whether the masterpieces are for a "high" tea or wedding reception or to be taken to someone as a special gift. Examples of this type are the Linzer Cookies, Pineapple Peek-A-Boos, Pineapple Cone Cookies, the decorative Checkerboard and Pinwheel Cookies and, of course, the cookies with their pretty "pressed" shapes.

Designed to delight the hearts of the youngsters and those who haven't forgotten the uninhibited joys of youth, the Molasses Dolls and the decorative "houses" are for those who have the time and patience to add trimmings that turn these cookies into fairy-tale magic, not just mere goodies to eat.

Outstanding for their flavor are the fragrantly flavored Anise Fingers, Caraway Triangles and Cardamom Cookies. If you haven't discovered what fun "seeds" can add to your baking, be sure you do soon. They have an appeal all their own.

Also flavor standouts are the Rum Chocolate Wafers, a sophisticated French combination—one that can go partying as often as a basic black dress.

A further word of encouragement about the Gingerbread and Puffed Cereal Houses. Actually a project like making a gingerbread or candy-bedecked house takes more time and patience than talent. It is not a job to be rushed. You'll find it time well spent, however, when you present one of these truly spectacular efforts at a child's birthday party or as a featured centerpiece at holiday time.

The directions are detailed and easy to follow. Try to picture in your mind beforehand what you will be doing. Read through the recipe and steps for putting a house together to be sure that all ingredients, trimmings and utensils are at hand. The rest is just a matter of going carefully through each stage until the last festive touch is placed on the completed scene. There is no reason at all why the process cannot be done over several days. The important thing is to allow yourself time for each step. That way the assembling and adding of finishing touches is fun.

Because such elaborate pieces are ordinarily made for decorative purposes, rather than to be eaten, you may wish to store yours away after use. The Gingerbread House made of rolled cookie dough keeps particularly well. Wrap it in tissue paper to protect the decorations, then overwrap in moisture-vaporproof wrapping before storing in a cool, dry place. The other houses may be kept (similarly wrapped) in a freezer from one season to the next. Of course, if they haven't had too prolonged exposure to air-borne dust, there is no reason at all why the youngsters shouldn't have the fun of consuming the sugar-plum visions. What an enjoyable way to celebrate New Year's Eve—after the decorative house has served its purpose over the holiday season!

If the house is to be part of a decorative "scene," it is most practical to build it on a tray or jelly-roll pan so that the total piece is easily transported and all the decorative additional pieces may be put in place once and for all.

Now on with the fun! It is really easier than you think. In this chapter are recipes for these Good Cookies:

PLAIN   FANCY

BALL

Baked Eggnog Rum Balls   Chocolate Cherry Balls
Black and White Balls   Date Bowlers
                                Peanut Butter Jewels

BARS

Rocky Road

LAYERED BARS

Chocolate Chip Dream Bars
Linzer Cookies
Pineapple Peek-A-Boos

PLAIN	FANCY

DROP

Crunchies	*Date Surprises*
	Pineapple Cone Cookies
	Turtle Pecan Cookies

FILLED

Mincemeat Turnovers

ICEBOX

Butter Nut Wafers	*Checkerboard Cookies*
	Checkerboard Squares
	Chocolate Pinwheel
	Cookies
	Date Pinwheel Cookies

PRESSED

Orange Cookies	*Chocolate Spritz II*

ROLLED

Molasses Dolls	*Anise Fingers*
(Gingerbread Men)	*Caraway Triangles*
Rum Chocolate Wafers	*Cardamom Cookies*

SPECIALTY BAKING

Gingerbread Cookie
House (Basic)
Gingerbread House (Mix)
Puffed Cereal House

Other recipes that could be included in this category are the following (to locate, see index):

BALL
  Scandinavian Tea Cookies
LAYERED BARS
  Almond Meringue Bars
  Layered Mocha Nut Bars
DROP
  Almond Kisses
  Fruit Lace Cookies
ICEBOX
  Anise Crisps
ROLLED
  Circus Mint Cookies
  Macaroon-topped Butter Cookies
  Picture Cookies
  Polish Tea Thins

BALL COOKIES

Baked Eggnog Rum Balls [PLAIN]

Very crisp and buttery

¾ cup butter
½ cup sifted powdered sugar
¼ cup brown sugar, firmly packed
1 egg

2 cups sifted all-purpose flour
¼ teaspoon salt
2 teaspoons rum
½ teaspoon vanilla

Cream butter thoroughly. Add powdered sugar, then brown sugar, mixing until well blended. Add egg. Stir in sifted flour and salt, gradually adding flavorings after part of the flour mixture is added. Form into ½-inch balls. Place on ungreased cookie sheet. Bake at 375 degrees until set, about 8 to 10 minutes. *Approximately 4 dozen*

Black and White Balls [PLAIN]

Easy to make

½ cup shortening
½ cup white sugar
½ cup brown sugar, firmly packed
1 egg
1 teaspoon vanilla

1¼ cups sifted all-purpose flour
2 teaspoons baking powder
1 teaspoon salt
1 cup rolled oats
1 6-ounce package semi-sweet chocolate bits

Cream shortening and sugars together well. Add egg and vanilla, blending until smooth. Sift together flour, baking powder and salt and add. Stir in rolled oats and chocolate bits. Shape dough into balls the size of a walnut. Bake on greased sheet at 350 degrees 12 to 15 minutes. *4 dozen*

Chocolate Cherry Balls [FANCY]

Nut-coated and cherry-topped fudgelike balls

½ cup butter or margarine
⅓ cup semi-sweet chocolate bits
16 large fresh marshmallows
2 cups sifted all-purpose flour

2 tablespoons water
1 teaspoon vanilla
1 cup uncooked rolled oats, quick or old-fashioned
1½ cups chopped nuts
18 candied cherries, cut in half

Combine butter or margarine, chocolate bits and marshmallows in saucepan or top of double boiler. Melt over low heat or hot water in double boiler, stirring to prevent scorching. When marshmallows are melted, stir in flour, water, vanilla and oats. Cool dough. Shape into small balls. Roll in chopped nuts and place half a candied cherry on top of each. Bake on ungreased cookie sheet at 325 degrees about 18 to 20 minutes. Cool on rack. *3 dozen*

Date Bowlers [FANCY]

Fruited centers

1 cup butter
½ cup sifted powdered
   sugar
1 teaspoon grated lemon
   rind
⅔ cup finely chopped nuts

2¼ cups sifted all-purpose
   flour
½ pound pitted dates,
   quartered
Sifted powdered sugar

Cream together soft butter and ½ cup powdered sugar. Add grated lemon rind. Mix nuts with flour and add to creamed ingredients gradually. Form a bit of dough around a quartered date for 1-inch diameter ball. Bake on ungreased cookie sheet at 400 degrees about 12 to 15 minutes. Roll cookies while hot in sifted powdered sugar. Cool. Roll again in sifted powdered sugar. *About 3 dozen*

Peanut Butter Jewels [FANCY]

Jelly-glazed

¾ cup shortening
½ cup peanut butter
½ cup brown sugar, firmly
   packed
1 egg
1 teaspoon vanilla

1¾ cups sifted all-purpose
   flour
¼ teaspoon baking powder
½ teaspoon salt
Apple, currant or raspberry
   jelly

Blend shortening and peanut butter. Cream in sugar gradually. Add egg and vanilla. Beat well. Sift together dry ingredients and stir in. Form dough in 1-inch balls. Place on ungreased sheet. With teaspoon or fingertip depress center of unbaked ball of dough. Bake 12 to 15 minutes at 350 degrees. Cool slightly. While warm, spoon a bit of jelly into centers. *3½ dozen*

BAR COOKIES

Rocky Road Bars [FANCY]

Rich, chocolate cookies with bits of marshmallow

2 ounces or squares un-
    sweetened chocolate,
    melted
½ cup butter or margarine,
    melted
2 eggs
1 cup sugar

¾ cup sifted all-purpose
    flour
½ teaspoon baking powder
¼ teaspoon salt
½ teaspoon vanilla
1 cup cut-up or miniature
    marshmallows
1 cup chopped nuts

Cool melted chocolate and butter. Beat eggs with sugar until light. Add cooled chocolate and butter. Sift together dry ingredients and stir in. Add vanilla, marshmallows and nuts. Pour into greased 9-inch-square pan. Bake at 350 degrees about 30 minutes. Cut into squares when cool. *3 dozen*

LAYERED BAR COOKIES

Chocolate Chip Dream Bars [FANCY]

Nutty-rich layered bars

Bottom Layer:
1 cup sifted all-purpose
  flour
2 tablespoons brown sugar
½ cup butter or margarine

Cut together until butter is in fine pieces. Press firmly in bottom of 8-inch-square pan. Bake at 350 degrees 15 minutes.

Top Layer:
2 eggs, well beaten
1½ cups brown sugar
¼ cup flour
½ teaspoon baking powder
¼ teaspoon salt

½ cup chopped nuts
1 6-ounce package semi-sweet chocolate bits
1 teaspoon vanilla

Beat egg and brown sugar. Sift together flour, baking powder and salt and fold in. Stir in nuts, chocolate bits and vanilla. Pour over baked mixture and bake 30 minutes more at 350 degrees. Cool before cutting into squares. *2 dozen*

Linzer Cookies [FANCY]

Apricot-jam-filled

3 cups sifted all-purpose
   flour
½ teaspoon baking soda
½ teaspoon salt
2 cups butter or margarine

6 egg yolks
Juice and grated rind of
   1 lemon
Apricot jam

Sift together dry ingredients and cut in butter, blending until mixture resembles coarse corn meal. Stir in egg yolks, lemon juice and rind. Spread two thirds of dough in 9 × 13-inch pan. Cover with apricot jam. Roll out remaining dough and cut in strips. Crisscross strips over top. Bake at 350 degrees 30 minutes. Cut into squares while warm. *4 dozen*

Pineapple Peek-A-Boos [FANCY]

Coconut-crusted layered bars

Bottom Layer:

1 cup sifted all-purpose
   flour
1 teaspoon baking powder
½ teaspoon salt

1 cup sugar
2 tablespoons butter or
   margarine
3 eggs

Sift together dry ingredients. Cut in butter to make small pieces. Beat eggs and add half to first mixture. Reserve other half for topping. Press into 9-inch-square pan. Cover with following:

Topping Layer:

1 cup crushed, drained
   pineapple
1 cup grated coconut

1 cup sugar
1 tablespoon melted butter

Combine in order given, blending in remaining half of

beaten eggs reserved from dough. Spread over unbaked bottom layer. Bake at 350 degrees 35 to 40 minutes or until top is firm and light brown. Cut into squares while warm. *3 dozen*

DROP COOKIES

Crunchies [PLAIN]

Crisp as caramel corn—with coconut, too!

1½ cups crushed cornflakes	½ cup shortening
¾ cup flour	2 tablespoons light corn
¾ cup sugar	syrup
⅔ cup grated coconut	1 teaspoon baking soda
½ teaspoon salt	½ teaspoon vanilla

Combine cereal, flour, sugar, coconut and salt in mixing bowl. Melt shortening over medium heat. Add corn syrup and cook and stir until mixture comes to a boil. Then add soda and stir rapidly to blend. When foam settles, remove mixture from heat at once, add vanilla and blend. Pour over dry ingredients. Mixture will be dry and crumbly. Press by tablespoonfuls against side of bowl and drop on ungreased baking sheets, placing cookies about 2 inches apart. Press with fork to flatten slightly. Bake at 375 degrees 7 to 8 minutes or until lightly browned. Cool 1 to 2 minutes, then remove cookies to rack with spatula. *2½ dozen*

Date Surprises [FANCY]

Easy party fare

1 pound pitted dates
4 dozen walnut halves
¼ cup butter or margarine
¾ cup brown sugar, firmly packed
1 egg

1¼ cups sifted all-purpose flour
½ teaspoon baking soda
1 teaspoon baking powder
¼ teaspoon salt
½ cup thick sour cream
1 teaspoon vanilla

Stuff dates with walnut halves. Cream butter and sugar well. Beat in egg. Sift together dry ingredients and add alternately with sour cream and vanilla. Add stuffed dates. Stir until well coated with batter. Drop on lightly greased baking sheet, one date for each cookie. Bake at 375 degrees about 10 minutes. Cool. *4 dozen*

Pineapple Cone Cookies [FANCY]

A child's delight

½ cup light corn syrup
½ cup butter or margarine
⅔ cup brown sugar
1 cup sifted all-purpose flour

¼ teaspoon salt
1 cup grated coconut
⅔ cup well-drained crushed pineapple

Combine corn syrup, butter and brown sugar. Bring to boil, and continue to boil, stirring frequently, until sugar is dissolved. Cool. Add flour and salt. Fold in coconut and pineapple. Drop on greased baking sheet, well apart. Bake at 325 degrees 10 to 12 minutes, just until cookies begin to brown. Let cool a minute before removing from baking sheet. Roll cookies into cones immediately after removal from baking sheet. If cookies become too stiff to roll, return to oven for a minute or two. *5 dozen*

Turtle Pecan Cookies [FANCY]

Chocolate-frosted treat

1 cup butter	1 teaspoon baking soda
1½ cups sugar	1 teaspoon salt
2 eggs	1 cup milk
3¾ cups sifted cake flour	1 teaspoon vanilla
2 teaspoons baking powder	½ pound large pecan halves

Cream together butter and sugar until light and fluffy. Add eggs and beat well. Sift together dry ingredients and add alternately with milk to creamed mixture. Add vanilla. Arrange pecan halves on lightly greased cookie sheet in the shape of a cross. Drop a teaspoonful of batter directly in center of the four nuts, being sure that batter covers the center tip of each. Bake at 375 degrees 10 minutes. Remove from sheet to rack to cool. Ice with frosting while cookies are still warm.

Frosting:

1 pound powdered sugar, sifted	2 ounces or squares unsweetened chocolate, melted
½ cup butter or margarine, softened	Top milk
1 teaspoon vanilla	

Mix sugar with butter, vanilla and melted chocolate. Stir in enough milk to make thin icing. Be sure icing is thin enough to cover the cookie portion completely.

FILLED COOKIES

Mincemeat Turnovers [FANCY]

Bite-size pies

½ cup soft shortening
1 cup sugar
2 eggs
2 tablespoons thick cream, sweet or sour
¼ teaspoon lemon extract

1 tablespoon grated lemon rind
2½ cups sifted all-purpose flour
½ teaspoon salt
¼ teaspoon baking soda
1½ cups thick mincemeat

Blend shortening with sugar. Add eggs, beating until smooth. Stir in cream, lemon extract and grated rind. Sift together dry ingredients and add. Chill 1 hour. Roll dough thin on lightly floured board. Cut in 2½-inch rounds or squares. Place 1 teaspoon mincemeat in center and fold dough over filling. Press edges together with fork tines or fingertips. Bake at 400 degrees about 10 minutes. *About 5 dozen*

Dough may be cut in small rounds and filling placed between two, sealing edges as above. Pierce center top with fork tines or slash for face design. Bake as above.

ICEBOX COOKIES

Butter Nut Wafers [PLAIN]

Delicately flavored

1¼ cups soft butter
1¼ cups sifted powdered sugar
¼ teaspoon salt

3 cups sifted cake flour
1 egg
1 tablespoon vanilla
1 cup finely chopped nuts

Cream butter and sugar until smoothly blended. Add salt

and 1 cup flour. Stir in egg and vanilla. Beat well. Add remaining flour and nuts. Shape dough into rolls. Chill 6 to 8 hours. Slice thin. Bake on ungreased sheet at 375 degrees 10 to 14 minutes. *4 to 5 dozen*

Checkerboard Cookies [FANCY]

Tea-party favorite

1 recipe plain dough for Ribbon Cookies (see index)

2 ounces or squares unsweetened chocolate, melted

Milk

Prepare dough according to recipe directions. Divide into three portions. Add melted, cooled chocolate to one portion. Chill all 2 hours. Divide one portion of plain dough and chocolate dough into 8 equal parts. Roll into thin rolls about the size of a pencil, then square by pressing with a knife or spatula. On lightly floured board, roll remaining portion of plain dough to large rectangular sheet the length of the small rolls of dough.

Brush center of rolled sheet of dough with milk. Lay alternating light and dark dough in 4 strips across the milk-brushed area of dough. Moisten top of this layer with milk lightly and place 4 more strips of light and dark doughs over bottom layer. Arrange light dough over dark, dark over light. Continue building layers until all dough is used. Brush exposed rolled dough with milk and press about the center block of dough. Wrap with waxed paper or foil. Chill overnight. Slice thin. Lay on very lightly greased cookie sheets. Bake at 375 degrees 8 to 10 minutes. *About 5 dozen*

Checkerboard Squares [FANCY]

Turn ribbons into squares

1 recipe plain dough for Ribbon Cookies (see index)	2 ounces or squares unsweetened chocolate, melted

Prepare dough according to recipe directions. Divide in two parts, adding melted, cooled chocolate to one. Prepare a small loaf pan (approximately 4 × 8 × 3) by lining smoothly with household foil or waxed paper. Divide white dough and press half into a smooth, even layer on bottom. Make second layer in same manner with half of chocolate dough. Repeat white layer and top with remainder of chocolate dough. Cover and chill 6 to 8 hours. Lift dough out of pan with paper. Cut into slices ¼ inch thick. Place four slices together so that light and dark dough layers alternate. Cut across stack for even ¼-inch slices. Lay squares on lightly greased sheet, pressing cubes together, if necessary. Bake until golden brown at 375 degrees 8 to 10 minutes. Avoid overbrowning. Cool on rack. *About 5 dozen*

Chocolate Pinwheel Cookies [FANCY]

Two flavors blend

1 recipe plain dough for Ribbon Cookies (see index)	2 ounces or squares unsweetened chocolate, melted Milk

Divide basic Ribbon Cookie dough into two portions. Add melted, cooled chocolate to one portion. Chill light and dark doughs 1 hour. Roll a portion of plain dough into rectangular sheet, trimming edges neatly. Roll chocolate dough into similarly sized sheet, trimming if necessary. Brush light dough sparingly with milk. Lay chocolate sheet on top. Roll dough as for jelly roll. Repeat process until all dough is used. Wrap rolls with waxed paper or aluminum foil and chill overnight. Slice rolls thin. Lay on very lightly greased cookie sheets. Bake at 375 degrees 8 to 10 minutes. *About 5 dozen*

Date Pinwheel Cookies [FANCY]

Toothsome treat

1 cup shortening	½ teaspoon salt
2 cups brown sugar, firmly packed	½ teaspoon baking soda
	4 cups sifted all-purpose flour
2 eggs	
1¼ teaspoons vanilla	

Gradually blend sugar into softened shortening. Beat eggs, add with vanilla. Sift together salt, soda and flour. Gradually add to creamed ingredients in three portions. Chill 4 hours. Roll out a third of dough at a time on lightly floured board. Spread each with a third of Date Nut Filling. Roll up as for jelly roll. Wrap in waxed paper or aluminum foil. Chill 6 to 8 hours. Slice. Place on sparingly greased cookie sheet. Bake at 400 degrees 10 minutes or until lightly browned. *About 10 dozen*

Date Nut Filling:

2¼ cups chopped, pitted dates	1 tablespoon lemon juice
1 cup sugar	1 cup finely chopped nuts (optional)
1 cup water	

Combine dates, sugar and water. Cook and stir until thick. Remove from heat. Add lemon juice and nuts. Cool.

PRESSED COOKIES

Chocolate Spritz II [FANCY]

Extra rich

⅓ cup shortening

2 3-ounce packages cream cheese

1 cup sugar

2 ounces or squares unsweetened chocolate, melted

1 egg

1½ teaspoons vanilla

½ teaspoon salt

½ teaspoon baking powder

2½ cups sifted all-purpose flour

Cream together shortening and room-temperature cream cheese until smooth. Gradually add sugar. Stir in melted, cooled chocolate. Beat in egg and vanilla. Sift together dry ingredients and add gradually. Form cookies with press on ungreased baking sheet. Bake at 375 degrees 8 to 10 minutes. *5 dozen*

Orange Cookies [PLAIN]

Flavor-fresh

1 cup butter

1 cup sugar

1 egg

1 tablespoon grated orange rind

1 tablespoon orange juice

2½ cups sifted all-purpose flour

½ teaspoon baking powder

Add sugar gradually to well-creamed butter, mixing smooth. Beat in egg, grated orange rind and orange juice. Sift flour with baking powder and stir in gradually, blending well. Form cookies with press on an ungreased sheet. Bake at 375 degrees 10 minutes or until lightly browned. Do not overbake or flavor will be impaired. *5 dozen*

ROLLED COOKIES

Anise Fingers [FANCY]

Brandy-flavored

2 cups sifted all-purpose flour
¼ teaspoon salt
1 teaspoon baking powder
⅔ cup sugar

¼ cup shortening
2 eggs
2 teaspoons brandy
1 tablespoon anise seed
Melted butter or cream

Sift together flour, salt, baking powder and sugar three times. Cut in shortening until well mixed but not greasy. Beat eggs well, add with brandy and anise seed to flour mixture. Turn out and knead on lightly floured board. Roll ¼ inch thick. Cut into bars 3 inches long and ½ inch wide. Place on lightly greased baking sheet. Brush top with melted butter or cream. Bake at 300 degrees until light golden brown, about 15 to 18 minutes. *3 dozen*

Caraway Triangles [FANCY]

Piquant with lemon rind

1 cup butter or margarine
½ cup sugar
1 tablespoon grated lemon rind
2 teaspoons cream

¼ teaspoon baking powder
¼ teaspoon salt
2 cups sifted all-purpose flour
Caraway seed

Stir sugar into soft butter. Add grated lemon rind and cream. Sift together baking powder, salt and flour, then add to mixture. Turn on floured board and knead lightly 15 seconds. Roll dough thin. Cut into triangles. Sprinkle caraway seed on top of cookies, pressing down lightly with fingertips. Bake on ungreased sheet at 350 degrees 15 minutes. *4 dozen*

Cardamom Cookies [FANCY]
Almond-garnished

⅓ cup butter
½ cup sugar
1 egg
¼ teaspoon salt
1 teaspoon baking powder

1⅓ cups sifted all-purpose flour
½ teaspoon crushed cardamom seed
Slivered, unblanched almonds

Cream butter, then blend in sugar. Add egg and mix smooth. Sift together dry ingredients, stir in cardamom and add to butter mixture. Chill dough 1 hour. Roll out a small portion of dough at a time, chilling remainder. Cut small circles and place on ungreased sheet. Brush top of cookies with milk or slightly beaten egg white and sprinkle with slivered, unblanched almonds. Bake at 400 degrees 8 to 10 minutes or until golden brown. *2½ dozen*

Molasses Dolls [PLAIN]
Such fun to decorate—good to eat, too!

½ cup butter
½ cup sugar
1 egg
½ cup light or dark molasses
2¼ cups sifted all-purpose flour

½ teaspoon salt
½ teaspoon baking soda
1 teaspoon baking powder
1 teaspoon ginger
1½ teaspoons cinnamon
½ teaspoon cloves
½ teaspoon nutmeg

Cream butter and sugar, then blend in egg and molasses. Sift together dry ingredients and add. Chill dough 2 hours. Roll out ⅓ inch thick on lightly floured board. Cut dolls with 6-inch cutter or use sharp knife to cut around cardboard patterns. Mouth and some details of dress may be drawn on dough with toothpick. Use currants and raisins for eyes, nose and buttons on clothes. Face may be formed on baked dough with decorating frosting, if preferred. Bake on lightly greased sheet 10 to 12 minutes at 350 degrees. *About 15 large dolls*

Dough may be rolled thin and cut with standard cookie cutters. Bake 8 to 10 minutes on lightly greased sheet at 400 degrees. *5 dozen*

Rum Chocolate Wafers [PLAIN]

French in origin but delicious in any language

1 recipe for Rolled Chocolate Dollars (see index)
1 tablespoon dark rum

Prepare Rolled Chocolate Dollars according to recipe directions, substituting rum for vanilla. Roll, cut and bake as directed. *6 dozen*

SPECIALTY BAKING

Gingerbread Cookie House [FANCY]

Basic rolled dough

1 cup shortening	1 teaspoon baking soda
1 cup sugar	1 teaspoon salt
1 cup molasses	1 teaspoon cinnamon
1 teaspoon vanilla	2 teaspoons ginger
5 cups sifted all-purpose flour	

Cream shortening and sugar. Stir in molasses and vanilla.

Sift together dry ingredients and add, mixing well. Work dough with hands to blend thoroughly. Divide dough in thirds. Roll dough out ¼ inch thick, rolling directly on baking sheet. Lay pattern of house on dough, cutting through doors and windows, but do not lift them from place. Remove trimmings and save. Use excess dough, rolled out ¼ inch thick, to cut Christmas motif cookies, as desired. Bake at 375 degrees 12 to 15 minutes or just until lightly browned. While hot, retrace outline of windows and doors and, if necessary, trim house edges to straighten. Cool on baking sheets, lifting out windows and doors. Assemble, using Decorative Icing to hold sides together. The icing becomes hard and will keep indefinitely. Join these first and let set. When firm, attach roof, one side at a time, then chimney and door. When frosting is firm, decorate with tinted Decorative Icing, tiny candies and silver dragees.

GINGERBREAD COOKIE HOUSE PATTERN

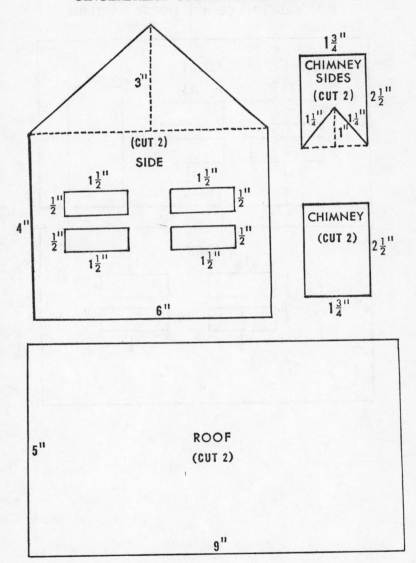

GINGERBREAD COOKIE HOUSE PATTERN

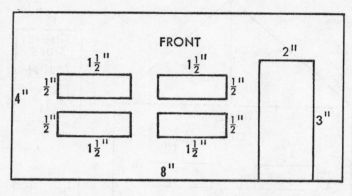

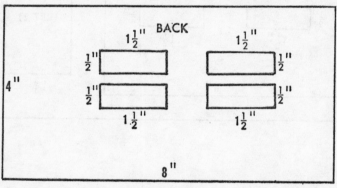

COMPLETED GINGERBREAD COOKIE HOUSE

Thick frosting not only cements sections together but provides snow for trimming. Decorate with tiny candies.

Gingerbread House [FANCY]

Made with a mix, baked in a form

   1 package gingerbread mix
   ½ cup sifted all-purpose
      flour
   ⅔ cup water

Combine ingredients and mix well. Pour into special cake-form pan, which has been well greased and floured. Spread batter evenly. Place pan on center rack in oven. Bake at 325 degrees 1¼ hours. Test by inserting toothpick in center. Remove end pieces and sides of cake-form pan. Cool on rack thoroughly. If bottom has bulged during baking, trim so that house sits level. Frost with Decorative Icing, which becomes hard and will keep indefinitely. Color part for trim lines.

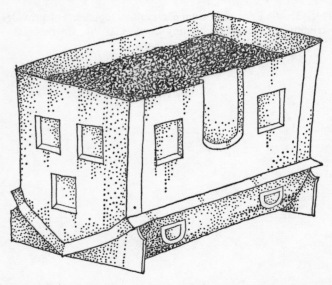

Special gingerbread house mold makes easy work of this gingerbread house. Form pan should be well greased and floured before adding batter. Put small sheet of aluminum foil on rack under pan, in case of leaks. Test by inserting toothpick in center to insure doneness.

Decorative Icing:

2 egg whites

⅛ teaspoon cream of tartar

2 teaspoons water

2½ to 3 cups sifted
powdered sugar

Beat egg whites, cream of tartar and water until frothy; gradually add powdered sugar. Beat until mixture holds soft peaks. Tint as desired with food coloring, dividing for more than one color. Use to frost house and also to decorate scene in which house is set. Use sugar cubes for chimney of house, inverted ice cream cones for fir trees. Icing may be put through decorating tube to form trim lines on house roof, windows and doors.

COMPLETED GINGERBREAD HOUSE

Decorative icing dries hard and keeps indefinitely. Divide recipe and tint to decorate different portions of the house. Roof, doors and windows are outlined with tip of cake decorator. Sugar cubes form chimney. Frosted, inverted ice cream cones form trees.

Puffed Cereal House [FANCY]

A family project

1 cup light corn syrup	1 teaspoon vanilla
¼ teaspoon salt	4½ cups Puffed Rice or
2 teaspoons vinegar	Rice Krispies
2 tablespoons butter or	
margarine	

Combine corn syrup, salt and vinegar. Cook to hard-ball stage. Remove from heat. Add butter and vanilla, stirring just to blend. Pour quickly over Puffed Rice, mixing as poured to coat evenly. With greased hands press into well-greased 8 × 12-inch pan. Make 5 batches as given above to make complete house.

1st Batch: Use entire batch for floor. Remove from pan after 3 minutes and cool on waxed paper.

2nd Batch: Cut long roof side, 7 × 9 inches, and cool as above. Then cut low house side from remaining slab, 2 × 5 inches.

3rd Batch: Cut short roof side, 7 × 7 inches, and high house side, 3 × 5 inches.

4th Batch: Cut house front, 6 inches high, 11 inches wide, then sloping down to 2 inches on one side and 3 inches on the other (see diagram). Cut window in front while still in pan.

5th Batch: Follow same diagram for back of house.

Cement sides to floor, then put roof in place, using Decorative Icing. Use toothpicks to hold in place while frosting sets. Spread roof with Decorative Icing and decorate with after-dinner mints laid overlapping to resemble tiles. Outline doors and windows with Decorative Icing, tinted red or green. Use chocolate bar, held in place by frosting, for door.

PUFFED CEREAL HOUSE PATTERN

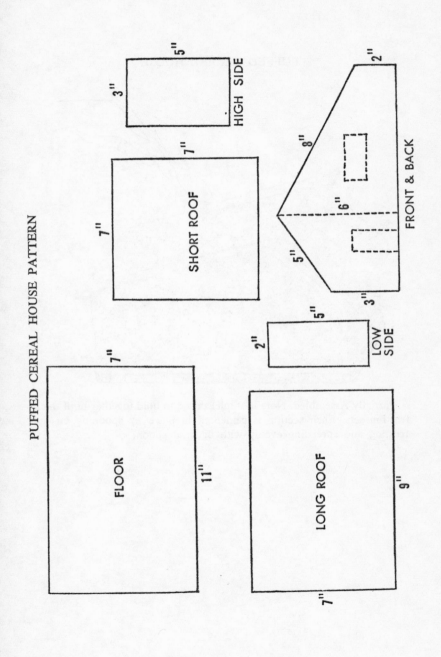

PUFFED CEREAL HOUSE

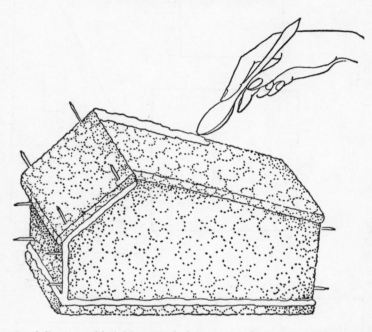

Partially Assembled. Note toothpicks used to hold together until thick frosting sets. Each section is cemented in place by spooning on the frosting and spreading evenly with back of spoon.

COMPLETED PUFFED CEREAL HOUSE

House is roofed with pink and green dinner mints. Doors and windows are trimmed with the same thick frosting which holds sections together. Edge windows with additional frosting tinted red. Decorate with tiny candies. Chocolate bar forms the door.

INDEX